Contents

Introduction

When you read on your own it is a very personal experience. You build a world in your imagination. You use the words of the writer to help you create a picture of what the people and setting look and sound like. Perhaps the writer tells you what a character is thinking or feeling, too. That world is yours – nobody else will ever be able to see it exactly as you do, even if they read the same novel themselves.

But with a play, the words on the page are just the starting point. They are not meant to simply be read and imagined – they are meant to be turned into a live performance. And although each of us will still have our own very personal idea of what the characters and the setting are like, taking a play from the script to the stage requires a group to imagine together. In a rehearsal room the actors and the director work together to bring the characters to life, to imagine what happened to them before the start of the play, and to explore what they are thinking and feeling. Before rehearsals start, the director and designers will begin to create the world of the play together starting with where the story happens and what the world of the play looks like. Even after this, the play isn't complete before an audience sees it, adding their collective imagination as well, to bring the story on stage alive.

The National Theatre is dedicated to making the very best theatre and sharing it with as many people as possible through: the theatres on the South Bank in London; touring and partnership productions; *NT Live* and *National Theatre: On Demand in Schools.*

At the National Theatre our rehearsal studios and workshops are constantly busy with actors, designers and directors working to bring plays to life – we produce around 25 each year. In a classroom you are studying a play, not making a production. But that doesn't mean you can't explore a play as actors, directors, designers and audience-members, thinking about the way you might approach a scene, or rehearsing different sections of the play to see how they change with different interpretations.

In this book you will find the text of the play that we produced at the National Theatre, together with images and resources which show you some of the ways the actors and production team worked to create our version of it. We hope this will inspire your own creative exploration of the play – which may be very different to ours. On the page, the play is just in one dimension. We hope you will enjoy bringing it to life.

Alice King-Farlow
Director of Learning
National Theatre

The play

Joey

6

Character list

Song Man
Song Woman
Lieutenant James Nicholls
(later Major)
Chapman Carter,
auctioneer (later Sergeant)
Albert Narracott
(later Private, then Lance-Corporal)
Arthur Narracott, Albert's uncle
Billy Narracott, Arthur's son,
Albert's cousin (later Trooper)
Ted Narracott, Albert's father,
Arthur's brother
Allan (later Sergeant)
Thomas Bone (later Trooper)
John Greig (later Trooper)
Rose Narracott, Albert's mother
Priest
Captain Charles Stewart (later Major)
Sergeant Thunder
(later Regimental Sergeant-Major)
Private David Taylor
Sergeant Fine
Soldier (Shaw), sentry
Soldier (Roberts), sentry
Geordie, sentry
Matron Callaghan
Annie Gilbert, a nurse

Martin, veterinary officer
Yeoman
Paulette
Emilie, Paulette's daughter
Private Schnabel
Private Klausen (later Lance-Corporal)
Captain Friedrich Müller
Soldier (Brandt)
Colonel Strauss
Dr Schweyk
German Soldier, in crater scene
Sergeant Klebb
Soldier (Franz)
Soldier (Jurgen)
Soldier (Schmidt)
Manfred
Soldier (Ludwig)
Baby Joey (Joey as a foal)
Joey
Goose
Topthorn
Coco
Heine
Villagers, German and British soldiers,
birds, etc.

Joey and Topthorn

Act 1

Scene 1
Devon – open country, 5 August 1912

Song Man emerges from the depths, with a sketchbook.

*Enter **Lieutenant James Nicholls**. **Song Man** gives him the sketchbook. He sketches the landscape, and it comes alive on the screen.*

Swallows. Screen turns to sky.

***Baby Joey** emerges. He calls out. He feeds himself. He investigates his vicinity. Everything is new. We get to know him.*

Scene 2
Continuous ('Auction scene')

Song: ***Only Remembered***

Song Man	Fading away like the stars in the morning Losing their light in the glorious sun Thus shall we pass from this earth and its toiling Only remembered for what we have done.

Villagers emerge. They will create a market.

Villagers	Only remembered, only remembered Only remembered for what we have done Thus shall we pass from this earth and its toiling Only remembered for what we have done…

Joey is corralled into a pen, in the foreground.

Song Man	Horses and men – ploughshares and traces The line on the land and the path of the sun Season by season we mark nature's graces Only remembered for what we have done.

Joey is fenced-in suddenly. Market hubbub.
Nicholls is at the pen. The hubbub diminishes
as he speaks.

*The **Villagers** come to teeming life, including*
***Chapman Carter**, the auctioneer. The pen*
*expands and the **Villagers** crowd around*
*it, including **Allan**, **Arthur Narracott**,*
Ted Narracott** (in the shadows), **Albert
***Narracott**, **Thomas Bone**, **John Greig** and*
***Billy Narracott**.*

Carter	Next lot: fifty-four: hunter colt! Half thoroughbred, half draught. His draught mother spent a night of passion with a thoroughbred, just like mine did!

Laughter.

Who'll start me off?! Twelve guineas, twelve guineas, do I hear twelve? Eleven? Gentlemen – he's a bit bony now, but he'll have some speed one day. Ten?

Allan	Ten.
Carter	Thank you, Mr Allan! Any advance, any advance?
Arthur	Eleven.
Carter	Mr Narracott, you're biddin'? Someone's movin' up in the world – do I hear twelve?

Nicholls has reappeared.

Nicholls	Twelve.

Carter	Lieutenant Nicholls, now we're talkin': he'll make a beautiful ridin' horse —
Arthur	Thirteen.
Nicholls	Fourteen.
Carter	Any advance, any advance?
Allan	Fifteen.
Carter	Lieutenant Nicholls, picture him gallopin' across your magnificent fields —
Arthur	Sixteen!
Nicholls	Seventeen.
Arthur	Eighteen!
Nicholls	Nineteen.
Arthur	Twenty!
Carter	Sir? —
Nicholls	I'm out, regrettably.
Carter	— Then it's with Arthur at twenty guineas – he must want a ridin' horse for young Billy there – you're sure, Lieutenant Nicholls?
Nicholls	Mr Narracott's determined; I won't stand in his way.
Carter	Twenty guineas, twenty guineas, any advance on twenty guineas? Congratulations, Mr Narracott, worth every penny. Going once, going twice —

From the shadows:

Ted	Twenty-one!

*The **Villagers** part for **Ted**.*

Albert	Father?

Carter   Ted Narracott bids twenty-one!

Arthur   Twenty-two.

Bone   Here we go: some Narracott strife.

Carter   Ted?

Bone puts his hand out to Greig.

Bone   John Greig: a pint says that horse is Arthur's.

Albert   Father?

Carter   With Arthur at twenty-two – going once —

Ted   Twenty-three.

Greig   *[Shakes]* Thomas Bone: it's Ted's.

Arthur   Twenty-four.

Billy   He's ours, Albert, he's mine!

Carter   Ted?

Ted   Twenty-five.

Albert   Are you sure about this, Father?

Arthur   Twenty-six.

Carter   With Arthur —!

Ted   Twenty-seven.

Arthur   Twenty-eight.

Ted   Twenty-nine.

Albert   What's Mother gonna say?

A moment; some reactions.

Arthur   Thirty.

Carter   Gentlemen! Thirty guineas for a hunter colt –
by my book that's a county record!

Ted   Thirty-one!

*Everyone looks to **Arthur**.*

Carter   Arthur —?

***Arthur** smiles.*

Arthur   Thirty-*three*.

Carter   Arthur…now, Arthur…I hope I don't need to remind no one that payment is required as soon as the hammer falls.

Arthur   Yer not suggesting I'm not good for it, Carter?

Carter   No, I'm not suggesting *you're* not: going once, going —

Ted   Thirty-four!

Arthur   Thirty-five.

Ted   Thirty-six!

Arthur   Thirty-seven.

Ted   Thirty-nine! Thirty-nine guineas!

*Everyone looks to **Arthur**.*

Carter   Arthur?

Greig   That pint is mine, Thomas Bone.

Bone   Arthur, don't stop now!

***Arthur** smiles. To **Ted**:*

Arthur   'E's all yours. Good luck, Ted.

Carter   Then it's with Ted Narracott at thirty-nine guineas! And for a hunter colt, that's unheard of in the parish, in Devon, and perhaps the whole of England!

Albert   Father, it's the mortgage money!

***Arthur** laughs as **Carter** brings things to a speedy conclusion, roping the foal and putting the rope in **Ted**'s hand.*

Carter	Going once, going twice, gone!

And we are at:

Scene 3
Ted and Rose's farm

*Rose Narracott is staring at **Ted**, **Joey**, and **Albert**. **Goose** is here.*

Rose	Ted? What in the name of hell are we gonna do with that?

Father and son are silent.

Say somethin', Ted. 'E's not even a proper farm horse, is he?

Albert	He's half thoroughbred, half draught – hunter.
Ted	Shut up, son.
Rose	I know he's a hunter – what good is a hunter to us? Can a hunter pull a cart, or pay the mortgage? The mortgage…tell me you paid the mortgage? Oh, no, Ted…how much?
Ted	*[Mumbled]* Thirty-nine guineas.
Rose	What?
Ted	Thirty-nine guineas.
Rose	Thirty-nine?! The pair of you should be locked up!
Albert	I didn't do it —
Rose	You didn't have nothin' to do with 'im buyin' this horse?
Ted	I bought him. I thumped Arthur. I wiped the floor with him!

*Ted ties **Joey** to a fence.*

Rose   What? What are you talkin' about? Oh, no…
no…Ted you never bid 'cause yer brother bid?
Ted?!

Ted   No, I wanted him.

Rose   A horse like that, Ted, what were you thinkin',
what are we gonna do?

Ted   You'll think of something, Rose. You always
do.

*Ted exits into the house. **Joey** is distressed.*

Rose   Ted! Ted!

Albert   *[To **Joey**]* Calm down, boy…calm down,
now…

Rose   You, young man, why didn't you do something
to stop him?

Albert   It all happened so quick…they just kept
shoutin'…before I knew it we were walkin'
home with it. Look how he holds his head.

Rose   Damn how he holds his bliddin' head, he's a
useless fathead!

Albert   I don't think he's a fathead.

Rose   Is he gonna fetch thirty-nine guineas at next
week's market?

Albert shakes his head.

Then tell me how he's gonna earn his keep?

Albert   I don't know.

Rose   Well, then. Nothin' to be done: we're just
going to have to get your father out of his
pickle again, you and me.

Albert How?

Rose I'm going to butter-up the bank manager, 'n'
       you are gonna bring him on. Yes you, Albert.
       You're doin all the chores: feedin', groomin',
       muckin' out, exercise.

Albert You mean we can keep him?!

Rose Till he's grown – then we sell 'im and pay the
      debt. If you hear strange noises from the house,
      don't worry, it's just me killin' yer father.

      Rose exits.

Scene 4
Continuous ('Trust scene')

Joey is still but curious.

Albert Right. Let's make a start, then.

       Albert tries to untie Joey. Joey reacts fearfully.

       It's all right! It's all right!
       You don't need to fear me. I won't hurt you.

       *Albert realises that Joey isn't comfortable with
       him coming near, so he loops the rope off him
       carefully and lets him run free.*

       Go on, then.

       *And we are in a field. Joey comes to rest.
       Albert looks at him and wonders what to do
       next. Of course! Feed him!*

       When was the last time you were fed? I bet you
       haven't had a thing all day.

       *Albert rushes off to get a bucket of food.
       Unwittingly he gives Joey an invitation to "join
       up" which Joey is looking for. So Joey starts to
       follow him off.*

Albert doesn't see this and comes running back into the space with his bucket of food to find Joey facing him and then suddenly stopping.

Joey looks at him suspiciously. But Albert is encouraged by what he took to be Joey's interest in the food.

No response.

Albert advances with the bucket. Joey backs off.

Come on. I won't hurt you…

Joey is still.

I promise I won't hurt you…I never will. It's oats, look.

Albert squats down, which is less threatening to Joey. He shows the food to Joey, who can smell it but doesn't want to approach. Sensing Joey's interest, Albert shows him what to do with food by pretending to eat it.

Mmmm. Mmmm. Good oats.

But Albert is still looking straight at Joey so Joey remains nonplussed. Albert suddenly realises that the horse might be scared of coming close to him, so he backs away and stands up facing Joey, giving him a double message that really confuses him (more space which feels good, coupled with full frontal facing which tells him not to advance).

Come on. Hello! I know you want it.

Frustrated, Albert wants to show Joey that he's messed up, so he decides to take away the food.

All right, suit yourself.

Albert goes back to the bucket, picks it up and walks away.

*Immediately **Joey** follows **Albert** and **Albert** senses it. He slows down and looks back at **Joey** who stops.*

*Albert realises that **Joey** doesn't like being faced directly. **Albert** backs towards him, muttering entreaties, and they meet. **Joey** feeds from the bucket.*

Good boy. Good boy…Go on then, get your

Baby Joey and Albert

nazzle into that.

Joey is relaxed. Albert senses it.

I bet you're missing your mother. First time away from her, I bet…but you're not alone, see? I'm here.

Albert reaches to touch Joey, but Joey flinches and tenses up.

Sorry…Sorry…

Albert gives Joey some space. Albert lets Joey feed.

What's your name then, eh? What d'you reckon? What shall we call you? Ranger? No? Howard? [Laughs] Hey?! Howard the horse?! – Joey?

Joey raises his head and Albert sees this.

Joey, eh! You like that one, eh? Joey, eh? You like the sound of that? [Joey snorts] You do, don't you? [Joey goes back to feeding] Hello, Joey. Joey boy. [Albert pets Joey] Hello. Hello. Joey.

Albert blows an owl whistle. Joey is startled for a second. Albert laughs.

When I whistle like that, you'll always know it's me, Albert.

Joey blows on Albert's face experimentally. Albert responds by blowing up Joey's nostrils.

That's a good start, Joey. That's a good start.

Scene 5
Continuous, then time passes
('Growing up scene')

*Enter **Song Man**.*

Song: **Snowfalls** *(Dialogue and song take place simultaneously.)*

*__Albert__ runs a short distance and turns to face **Joey**. He calls him with the whistle. He whistles again. **Joey** won't approach because the boy is facing him.*

Song Man And I'll wager a hat full of guineas
Against all of the songs you can sing —

*__Albert__ crouches down facing away from **Joey** and whistles again. This time he comes.*

That some day you'll love and the next day you'll lose
And winter will turn into spring —

*__Joey__ and **Albert** exchange a nose blow.*

Albert Clever boy, Joey lad. Who's a smart boy?

__Joey__ springs away.

*Winter: February 1913. Snow. **Albert** learns to groom **Joey**. **Joey** is stronger and more coordinated.*

Song Man And the snow falls, the wind calls
And the year turns round again —
And like Barleycorn who rose from the grave —
A new year will rise up again.

*__Joey__ has run some distance. He waits for **Albert**, who catches up and celebrates their togetherness.*

__Albert__ somersaults into summer: June 1913.

But there will come a time of great plenty
A time of good harvest and sun
Till then put your trust in tomorrow, my friend
For yesterday's over and done —
Ploughed, sown, reaped and mown
And the year turns round again —

*__Albert__ lies down with his hat over his face.
__Joey__ goes to him and nudges it off with his
nose.*

Albert   Get off. You silly donkey.

Song Man   And like Barleycorn who rose from the grave —
A new year will rise up again.

*Rain. __Albert__ puts a sugar cube in one hand
and holds both arms out with clenched fists.*

Albert   All right, you think you know everything?
There's no way you'll know which hand it's in.

__Joey__ finds the sugar cube.

Eh, you got me! Good boy, Joey. Good boy.

*__Joey__'s enthusiasm builds into a rear. __Albert__ is
delighted. He can't believe the playfulness and
athleticism of his horse.*

Hello? What's that, then? Do that again! And
whey up, boy!

*__Albert__ tries to train __Joey__ to rear up again
by jumping himself. He puts all his horse-
whispering skill into the effort.*

*__Joey__ does nothing in response. He is entirely
still. Then he runs with an explosion of energy.*

*__Albert__'s idea: "I'll watch him like a hawk – and
the next time he rears I'll give him the signal
at the same time so he'll learn to associate the
signal with the rear."*

*Joey rears again and **Albert** catches him with the signal.*

And whey up, boy! Good boy, Joey!

*Joey picks up on **Albert**'s excitement and goes capering into the field.*

*Albert chases him, desperate to settle him and try it for real. Has the lesson truly gone in? Albert gets **Joey** to settle. He gives him the cue. Joey responds with a rear.*

*It's worked! **Albert** is a horse trainer! The best moment of his life!*

*Albert rewards **Joey** with a lovely nuzzle so Joey will never forget this. One more, just to cement it, so **Joey** will be able to rear on cue whenever **Albert** wants.*

Albert gives the cue —

And whey up, boy!

*— and at the top of his rearing up, **Baby Joey** makes way for grown **Joey**, so it is grown **Joey** whose front hooves hit the ground – and two years have passed. It is July 1914.*

Song Man   Phoebe arise
A gleam in her eyes
And the year turns round again —
And like Barleycorn who rose from the grave —
A new year will rise up again.

Albert   All right, you ready for a ride then? Yeh! C'mon!

*Joey takes **Albert** on his back.*

*Exit **Joey** and **Albert**. Walking, into a trot, into a glimpse of a gallop.*

Scene 6
A path bordering Ted and Rose's farm, early evening, 29 July 1914 ('Muybridge scene')

*Music continues. Enter **Nicholls**. He sketches. Image comes to life on the screen.*

*Enter **Billy**, urging on **Arthur**.*

Billy   Up here, Father.

Arthur   Where?

Billy   Wait, Father, they'll come. Every evenin' they – *[Sees them]* – there!

Horse in motion on the screen.

Arthur   Bleedin' hell.

Billy   See how he growed up?! He looks like a proper hunter, don't he?

Arthur   Let's see how he goes, first. Looks aren't everythin'…

***Albert** gallops on **Joey**. He's whooping with the sheer joy of it.*

Aren't you a beauty!

The galloping sequence ends.

*Enter **Ted**. **Arthur** and **Billy** were not expecting to see him.*

Ted   Arthur.

Arthur   Evenin', Ted.

Ted   What're you doing 'ere?

Arthur   Just seen young Albert tearin' up the

countryside on that 'orse.

Ted Get off my land, the pair of you.

Arthur You must be dyin' to sell him by now. You'll never get back what you paid for him though, will you?

*Arthur laughs. So does **Billy**.*

Ted That horse is the best purchase you never made, Arthur.

Arthur Nothin' but a plaything for young Albert – what's the point of that, on this little swamp of a farm?

Ted He's more than that…I don't need to sell him…Joey'll earn his keep.

Arthur A hunter?

Ted I'll work 'im hard.

Arthur Work 'im?!

Ted Come autumn, he'll be ploughin' and harrowin'.

Arthur Ploughin'?! I'd like to see you try to make that ridin' horse plough!

Ted You wait and see. I'll turn him into a good farm horse, you bet yer life on it.

Arthur Would you bet the horse on it?

A moment.

Billy and me are on our way to The George for a drink, Ted. Can I buy you one?

Ted Evenin', Arthur.

Arthur Someone's scared of a little bet. He always was a shirker when it came to a fight, Billy.

Ted	I ain't scared of nothin', and I ain't walked away from a fight in my life.
Arthur	So that's a yes to a drink?

*Exit **Arthur** and **Billy**. **Ted** follows.*

*Enter **Albert** and **Joey** – their symbiotic relationship is complete – and we are at:*

Scene 7
Ted and Rose's stables, shortly after ('Chickens scene')

*Enter **Goose**.*

Albert	Good boy, Joey. Good boy. You were born for that, Joey. Born for it. What's that then? We was born for each other. Soppy bugger. Come on Joey, let's get you in.

***Albert** stables **Joey**.*

	I'll groom you up all clean and shiny, Joey, I will. You like that don't you, c'mon?

***Albert** grooms **Joey**. Enter **Rose**, unnoticed.*

Rose	And how are the chickens doing, Albert?
Albert	Hello, Mother. The chickens? The chickens are grand.
Rose	You didn't feed 'em, did you?
Albert	I will…I promise…after supper…
Rose	It's too late, son. They've departed this life.
Albert	*[A bombshell]* What? All of them?
Rose	You know, yer father took out the mortgage for me and for you. Everythin' counts, chickens 'n' all – you let this farm go to pieces, we do too, you understand?

Albert	Yes, Mother.
Rose	Good lad. Don't worry, I'm teasin', I fed 'em.
Albert	Mother!
Rose	And look at Joey – that is what I call the peak of health. You have done well with him. I am proud of you, son.
Albert	Thanks.

Rose squeezes **Albert**'s muscles.

Rose	'N' you've come on and all.
Albert	Get off.
Rose	He'll fetch a good price. Well…come in. Supper's ready. And wash your hands.

Rose exits indoors.

Albert	It ain't never happenin', Joey. I'll find a way ta keep you. I'll talk her into it…or I'll pay the debt myself if I have to. We'll never sell you, Joey, never. Good night, Joey. Good night.

Albert exits indoors.

Scene 8
The same, later that night.
('Stables scene')

*Enter **Ted**, drunk.*

***Goose** attacks him; Ted drives **Goose** off.*

Ted   Shhhh, shhhhhh…

Come on, Joey, let's get the collar on yer.

***Ted** tries to place the collar over **Joey**'s head, **Joey** evades the collar three times.*

Don't mess me about.

***Ted** goes for **Joey** and **Joey** knocks the collar out of **Ted**'s hands with his nose. **Joey** screams, turns away. **Ted** looks back towards the house, goes back for collar and **Joey** stops him by kicking in his direction.*

You choose; kind words or cruel whip.

***Ted** goes for collar again, **Joey** rears, **Ted** falls down, as **Ted** gets up, **Joey** spins 'round lifts his hind leg in warning, completes rotation and faces **Ted**.*

Choose cruel whip an' I'll whop you till you're bleedin'. *[**Ted** gets the whip]* Right then, 'ave it your way, *[**Ted** goes after **Joey** with the whip]* take that – and that, and that.

***Ted** whips **Joeys** on his right side, **Joey** turns, **Ted** hits him on his left, and hits him again.*

*On the third whip **Joey** advances on **Ted**, pushing **Ted** back and then **Joey** kicks him with his front leg, knocking **Ted** to the ground. **Albert** enters. **Joey** backs into stable.*

Albert	No! No…Joey!

Albert comes between Joey and Ted and tries to calm Joey down.

Ted	Get out of my way!
Albert	No!

Ted whips Albert. Albert recovers and stares.

Don't you ever come near 'im again.

Enter Rose.

Rose	What's going on?
Albert	He was whippin' Joey!

Albert goes to Joey.

Ted	I have to teach that horse to plough.
Rose	What are you talkin' about?
Ted	Plough, Rose, plough.
Rose	How much have you had to drink?
Ted	I've made a bet.
Rose	What?
Ted	A good bet.
Rose	*[Realisation dawning]* Oh, no…
Ted	With Arthur, Rose, that's right.
Rose	How much is at stake?
Ted	Well, if I win —
Rose	You won't! —
Ted	The price we paid for him – thirty-nine guineas!
Rose	What if you lose?

Ted	I'll win!
Rose	Answer me, Ted – if we lose?
Ted	The horse.
Albert	*[Tears out of the stables]* No! No! No, Father. That's not fair!
Ted	That horse will plough.
Albert	He can't.
Ted	He's got a whole week to learn.
Albert and Rose	A week?!
Rose	He won't plough in a year! He's a riding horse, you've lost him, Ted, we've lost him!
Albert	Stupid, stupid bet!
Ted	Don't you dare talk to me like that.

Ted goes for Albert; Rose steps in between them. Joey is extremely agitated.

Rose	Both of you, stop it!

Albert rushes back to calm Joey. But the horse, reading Albert's emotions, will not settle. Joey continues to respond to Albert as the scene continues.

Albert sings to comfort Joey.

Ted	Albert: you 'ave to teach that horse to plough.
Albert	I can't. It'll hurt him.
Ted	No?
Albert	No.
Ted	Then Arthur can have 'im with a bullet in his head.

Ted walks off.

Albert and Joey

Rose   Ted!

Albert   You'll have to shoot me first, you coward.

*Ted stops, back to **Albert**.*

That's what they call you! It's what everyone
says, you drink 'cause you never was a soldier
in South Africa 'cause you're a coward!!

Ted continues into the house. A moment.

Rose	Ted. Ted.

*Ted continues into the house. This is **Albert**'s last chance.*

Albert	All right…all right, I'll do it…

Ted turns.

Ted	In one week?
Albert	*[Nods]* One week.
Ted	Good. *[To **Rose**]* So that's that then. The boy'll turn him into a farm horse, and everythin' will be all right.
Rose	You ain't goin' indoors till yer sober.

Ted makes to leave.

Albert	Father!

Ted stops.

If we win, we don't sell Joey. 'Cause then he'll earn his keep. Joey's mine, Father. You have to give me your word. Do you?

Beat.

Rose	Ted?
Ted	I give you my word. I'd have fought in that war if I could have. I stayed to look after the Narracott farm. We're here today and Arthur has a roof over his head because I stayed. I'm no shirker.

Ted grunts assent and exits into the darkness.

Rose	One week? A ridin' horse, one bleedin' week?
Albert	How, Mother?
Rose	I dunno, son. I suppose you're just gonna have to find a way. 'Cause if you lose Joey, we lose

everythin'. I can't go back to that bank again, Albert…there's no more goodwill for us in the village, none.

Albert can't answer.

So…I'll do your chores. You don't need to worry about no chickens. You just make sure this stupid…stupid…hare-brained…stupid, stupid —

Albert hugs her.

Albert I'll do it, Mother.

Perhaps she doesn't believe him, but grabs him.

Rose All right, then. So. Start early. Don't waste no time.

Albert I can do it Mother, do you believe me?

Rose *[Nods]* Good lad. One more thing. Stop growin' up.

Albert half smiles. Rose exits indoors.

Scene 9
Continuous, then time passes, evening 29 July ('Learning to plough scene')

Albert That was devilish stupid, wasn't it? If you want to survive, Joey, you've got to learn that you're never to kick anyone ever again. Now I am gonna teach you to plough and you're gonna learn. Understood? 'Cause then we can be together for ever, which is the way I believe things are meant to be. What do you think of that? You believe that, too, don't you? We got seven days, Joey. Just seven days. So we'll start with the collar.

Day One: 30 July.

It's all right, this. It's just a bit of old leather. It's all right in't it? Joey it's all right. Easy Joey…

Joey shies when Albert tries the collar on him.

Stop that! You're just going to have to learn to take it. I'm talking to the draught horse part of you now – the calm, sensible part. Let's try and leave the thoroughbred part of you out of this.

Albert kneels down with his back to Joey and makes an owl call. Albert puts the collar around his neck and Joey responds to the owl call by walking to Albert. Joey reluctantly accepts the collar from Albert.

Enter Song Man: music under.

Well done, Joey! Well done!

Song: **Brisk Ploughboy**

Song Man   It's of a brisk young ploughboy,
He was a-ploughing on the plain
And his horse it stood down in yonder shade
It was down in yonder glade he went whistling to plough —

Albert leaves the stable and owl-calls for Joey to follow. The stable melts away.
Day Two: 31 July. Over the coming days, Rose assists Albert in his task.

And by chance there he met a pretty maid, pretty maid
By chance there he met a pretty maid.

Albert   Six days left. Joey, six. Ploughing bridle and reins.

Albert puts the bridle on Joey and clips the reins on.

Song Man   And oft times they wandered to that yonder glade
And contented they lay amidst the shade
And the sweet bells, they did ring and the nightingale did sing
All for the ploughboy and his tender maid, tender maid
All for the ploughboy and his tender maid.

Albert teaches Joey to understand the reins. Music under.

Albert   You've got to feel me now Joey, feel me. And round to the left. To the left. That's it, boy. To the right. Good boy. Good boy, Joey.

Rose   Good boy…

Albert   All the way, Joey. Straighten up, Joey. Good boy. Well done, Joey. Well done. Whoa!

Day Three: 1 August.

Five more days. Today you're going to pull me.

Rose attaches the traces.

Song Man   But when her cruel parents they did come to know
That her love he was a-ploughing on the plain
They sent for the press-gang
And pressed her love away
They sent him to the war to be slain.

Joey is now in the traces. Albert attempts to teach him to pull.

Albert   Go on, Joey. Walk on. Walk, Joey, walk.

*Ad lib entreaties till **Rose** grabs **Joey** by the bridle:*

Rose   Move it, you beast!

***Joey** misreads **Albert** and **Rose** and backs up dangerously. **Albert** has to shout to stop him. Things are going badly.*

No, no, no! Albert!

Song Man   They sent for the press-gang
And pressed her love away
They sent him to the war to be slain.

*During this stanza **Goose** has irritated **Joey** who has pulled a little and by accident. **Albert** doesn't know if he has learned his lesson or not:*

Albert   Do you think that went in, Ma? Did it?

Rose   I hope so, son.

Albert   So do I, boy, 'cause we ain't got no time to do it again.

Day Five: 3 August.

Three days left, Joey. The plough. It's easy this, Joey. Back up, Joey. Back up.

***Albert** takes off the traces and gives them to **Rose**, who exits. He attaches the plough.*

Song Man   And when he was upon the sea
His love on England's shore
He swore by every star that rose on high
He would never to the ploughing go
Lest she be at his side
Together and for ever by and by, by and by
Together and for ever by and by.

Joey and the Goose

Albert	Come on. Yeh! Walk on, Joey. Yeh! Dig in! Dig! Pull! Yeh!

Joey is making no progress. After three attempts he gives up and stands impassively.

You ain't even trying!

Joey kicks the plough.

Day Seven: 5 August. Enter Billy, furtively.

Albert	It's our last day and you haven't even bloody ploughed yet. Come on. Yeh! Walk!

*Joey's hindquarters sink, which will enable him to pull. **Albert** notices.*

You're getting it, you're getting it. Walk on Joey. Walk!

*With the unfamiliar act of pulling, **Joey** falls.*

Whoa! Whoa! Get up! Get up, Joey! It's all right. You've got to get up! You don't know Joey, so I'm going to have to do the knowing for you…but the rest of your life depends on this. So you get set to pull, eh?

Scene 10
A field continuous; dawn,
Wednesday 5 August 1914
('Ploughing scene')

(War was declared by the Prime Minister Herbert Asquith and Cabinet in London at 11 p.m. on Tuesday 4 August.)

***Goose** stalks **Billy**, and flushes him out of hiding.*

Billy	Go away, no, no, go away, go away…

***Billy** trips, **Goose** flies off.*

Albert	Are yer spying, Billy Narracott?
Billy	Waitin' for Father.
Albert	"Waitin' for Father."
Billy	Enjoy your last few minutes with my horse – and your farm.
Albert	I'll kill you before I let you get Joey.

Billy	I'd like to see you try.
Albert	That little goose put the wind up you! That's a sign of a coward if ever I saw one!
	*As they stand off, enter **Carter**, **Greig**, **Bone**, **Allan**, **Arthur**, **Ted** and **Rose** (and other **Villagers** to watch the ploughing, including the village **Priest**).*
Arthur	Billy – come 'ere!
Ted	Albert!
Bone	Ted, you're lookin' a little pale.
Greig	Do you need a pint?
Ted	No, I don't need no pint.
Carter	All right everyone, let's get this over with then we can all go home for breakfast.
Arthur	*[With buckets as markers]* Let the horse plough from 'ere… *[Puts first bucket down]* to… *[Walks some distance with second bucket]*
Allan	To Timbuktu, eh Arthur?
	Others laugh.
Ted	*[Taking bucket]* To 'ere.
Carter	Split the difference.
Ted	*[Not very far]* To here then.
Arthur	That ain't the difference. To 'ere.
Carter	Agreed?
Arthur and Ted	Agreed.
Ted	Well, you can see my stake standin' right there in front of you Arthur. Where's yours?
Arthur	*[Producing cash]* Thirty-nine guineas.

Carter	Ted Narracott bets the 'orse, Arthur Narracott thirty-nine guineas!

Carter snatches the money out of Arthur's hand and gives it to the Priest.

Arthur	Eh, Carter —!
Carter	Reverend will look after it. All right, everyone? Albert, when yer ready.

Joey lines up.

Rose	Good luck, the pair of you.
Bone	[Hand out to Greig for a bet] John Greig, that horse won't plough.
Greig	Thomas Bone, I agree: that horse won't plough.
Albert	C'mon Joey. It's all right. C'mon Joey! Good boy! Dig in, Joe! Walk on!

Joey starts to pull but veers off the straight line. Albert immediately shouts:

Whoa!…

Joey stops.

Arthur	I've won! Billy, he's yours!

Some people in the village think this is so.

Albert	No, wait…no, no, no. False start, false start!
Ted	[Simultaneously] False start, false start!
Priest	He's right – false start. The plough hasn't cut yet.
Carter	If the reverend says so, we go again!

Lines overlap:

Ted	Hasn't cut, hasn't cut —

Billy   Not fair!

Arthur   It hasn't cut 'cause it can't cut —!

*And then **Joey** sets off; **Villagers** react: "Look!", etc.*

Albert   Go on, Joey. Go on, Joey. That's it, Joey. Go on.

Song: **Rolling Home.**

Dialogue during song:

Rose   Come on, Joey, come on, boy! Good boy, good boy…

Ted   Go on, Joey. Go on, boy. Do it, boy.

*Etc. The **Villagers** start rooting for Joey.*

Song Man and Villagers

Round goes the wheel of fortune
Don't be afraid to ride
There's a land of milk and honey
Waits on the other side
There'll be peace and there'll be plenty
You'll never need to roam
When we go rolling home, when we go rolling home
Rolling home,
When we go rolling home
When we go rolling, rolling
When we go rolling home.
Rolling home,
When we go rolling home
When we go rolling, rolling
When we go rolling home!

*As the song climaxes **Joey** succeeds in ploughing the furrow. Cheers.*

Ted   Yes! Yes!

Albert   How did you do that? What a beautiful boy!

Carter   Well, that was a bloody miracle.

Rose   Well done, well done, Joey! And well done, Albert!

Albert   What a team we make! Joey and Albert together forever.

Billy   Father, you said 'e was mine! You said he'd never do it!

Arthur   Clear and sheer fluke.

Rose   Not true, Arthur. Albert won fair and square. Ain't that right, Ted?

*Ted snatches the money out of the **Priest's** hands:*

Ted   Thank you, reverend. Eh look, Arthur. Thirty-nine guineas *and* the horse – both mine!

Rose   No, the horse is Albert's, and this *[Snatches money from **Ted**]* is the mortgage money.

*Some laughter at **Ted**. **Ted** grabs **Rose** and hugs her as:*

A peal of church bells stops everyone in their tracks. The date appears on the screen.

Carter   You all know what that means. The German Kaiser has refused to withdraw his troops from Belgium. The British Empire is now at war with Germany!

Enthusiastic crowd reaction – then pick out both sides of the Narracott family.

Albert   Yer mine now, boy…

Rose   Ted…?

Ted   Those devils.

Albert   Yer all mine.

Arthur   Those are the last bells we'll hear till we've pushed them back where they belong!

End bells.

Carter   All men in the Yeomanry prepare to be mobilised!

Rose   C'mon, Albert, hurry now…

*Rose urges off **Albert**, **Joey**, and **Ted**.*

Rose   Albert…c'mon, Albert…

*Exit **Rose**, **Ted**, **Albert** and **Joey**.*

Scene 11
Village green, 11 August 1914 ('Mustering/Sequestering scene')

*The sequestering and muster – a gathering of men and horses. Military music. Flags. **Carter** and **Allan** become Sergeants.*

*Nicholls – now **Major Nicholls** – joins them for a formal photograph.*

*Enter **Topthorn**, bearing **Captain Charles Stewart** in dress uniform, serving as the recruiting image.*

Song: *Scarlet and the Blue*

All   Then hoorah for the Scarlet and the Blue
With the helmets a-glittering in the sun
And the bayonets flash like lightning
To the beating of a military drum.

Allan   Your king and country need you! Join up to the Royal Devon Yeomanry!
New recruits here!

***Billy** has been marched on by **Arthur**.*

Billy	But, Father, I don't want to…
Arthur	Hush, Billy, don't shame me.

*Enter **Ted**.*

Carter	Horses, fine horses, bring them along! Your country needs *them*, too. And we pay fair. Forty pounds for a trooper's mount, one hundred for an officer's!

*Photo flash and all freeze except **Ted**.*

Ted	How much?
Carter	One hundred pounds.
Song Man	I was once a jolly ploughboy I was ploughing of the fields all day —
Carter	Ted?
Song Man	When a sudden thought came to my mind —

*Exit **Ted** and all unfreeze.*

Allan	Who wants the King's shilling? Join up, join up! Attestation forms over there!
Carter	Billy Narracott – you're nineteen?
Arthur	He's nineteen.
Carter	John Greig, Thomas Bone! – you signing as troopers?
Greig	Yes, Sergeant!
Bone	To the Front!

*Their enthusiasm contrasts with **Billy**'s unease.*

Carter	Good men – you take the shilling, they pay me sixpence, we're all happy. Read the form, sign it –

***Billy** is flustered (he can't read).*

– it's just the oath, lad: you swear that you'll be faithful to His Majesty King George the Fifth, so help you God. Don't you worry, you'll sort those Germans out, it's the Kaiser who needs God's help, 'cause we're gonna push him right out of Belgium, back into Germany, through Germany and out the other side, and be home in time for tea!

All cheer. Photo flash. All freeze.

Arthur and Billy move away from Carter. Arthur presents Billy with a knife.

Billy   Father, I'll work hard. I don't want to go to France.

Arthur   Don't worry. You'll be all right. I'm too old, this time I'll stay for the farm. I've something for you. *[Arthur takes out a knife]* Your grandfather's knife. He carried it in Afghanistan in 1878, and then it was mine, in South Africa. You look after this and it'll look after you, and if you ever have cause to use it, me and your grandfather will be guiding your hand. Well, goodbye.

Allan   Trooper Narracott, *[All unfreeze]* you'll be orderly to Captain Stewart, over here.

Photo flash. All freeze.

Song Man   And I've leaved behind my Molly
She's the girl that I adore
And I wonder if she'll think of me…

Enter Ted, pulling Joey.

Ted   Come on, Joey, Come on. I know, I know, I ain't Albert…c'mon, you bugger…

Music starts and all unfreeze.

All	And the bayonets flash like lightning to The beating of a military Beating of a military Beating of a military drum.
Ted	Major Nicholls?
Nicholls	Yes.
Ted	Edward Narracott, sir.
Nicholls	Volunteering him?
Ted	I'm doing my bit, sir. I paid a record price fer him.
Nicholls	Yes, I remember.
Ted	Now he's the finest horse in the parish.
Nicholls	I've seen his paces – but it's not you who rides him out is it?
Ted	*[Shakes head]* No, no sir, that's my boy. I ain't got long, sir. An officer's horse, I'd say.
Nicholls	You would, would you?

Sergeant Carter admires Joey – aware, of course, of what Ted has done.

Carter	No splints, no curbs, good feet and teeth. Sound as a bell, sir.
Nicholls	A hundred pounds, then.
Carter	One hundred.
Ted	Thank you, sir.

One hundred pounds is counted into his outstretched hand. Enter Albert.

Albert	Father! Father! Father! You've sold him? You've sold Joey to the army? Joey's my horse!
Ted	A hundred pounds.

*Enter **Rose**.*

Albert	But he's mine – I won the ploughin'!
Rose	Albert!
Nicholls	Steady on, young man.
Albert	*[To **Rose**]* He's sold him to the army —
Ted	A hundred pounds, Rose —
Albert	You promised Father! You promised!
Rose	Ted, what are you doing…?
Albert	Father, please, please – I promise I'll never defy you again and he'll never kick you ever again —
Ted	No, no, he's never kicked me —
Albert	— Yes he did…
Ted	Shut up, boy.
Albert	That's right! That means he's not right for the army, don't it? He's got a nasty streak! He kicked me*!*

Albert begins to take *Joey* away.

Nicholls	Young man. Come here. That's an order: come!

*Photo flash. Freeze all except **Nicholls**, **Albert** and **Joey**.*

Nicholls	Now, then. Albert, is it?
Albert	*[Nods]* Sir…
Nicholls	Has Joey kicked you? Has he?

Albert shakes his head.

And has he a nasty streak?

Albert	*[Shakes head]* He is spirited, but that's the best thing about him.
Nicholls	I thought so.
Albert	If Joey's goin' I'm goin' too. I'm volunteerin'.
Nicholls	How old are you?
Albert	Nineteen.
Nicholls	Is that the truth?
Albert	*[Beat; the head shake again]* Sixteen.

*Photo flash and all re-position into a new freeze except **Albert**, **Joey** and **Nicholls**.*

Nicholls	Joey's quite a horse, isn't he? I've seen you riding him, and I've sketched him. I'll show you someday. We could do with men like you, Albert, you're spirited the way he is, but you're not old enough – so your place is at home with your father, and Joey's is with the army. You have my word as an officer that he'll be well cared-for. He'll be my mount, so I'll care for him myself. That's a promise.
Albert	But how long will he be gone?
Nicholls	A few months at most. We have to nip this threat in the bud, Albert. The Germans are already in France, and if we don't stop them now, who knows where they'll go next? You're helping us to bring this war to a swift end.
Albert	And then I can buy him back, sir? After it's over?

***Nicholls** struggles with his answer. **Stewart** steps forward breaking his freeze:*

Stewart	You can buy him back.

Photo flash; all unfreeze.

Nicholls	Captain Stewart!
Stewart	Sir.

A moment.

Nicholls *[To Albert]* Say goodbye to him now.

Albert Now, sir? Right now?

Nicholls Say goodbye, Albert.

Albert Joey. Joey boy…I promised I'd never let anything bad happen to you…but you have to go away with that man there…he's called Major Nicholls…and he's promised we'll be together again. So you do yourself proud in France, Joey. You drive those Germans out, then you come home, it's just a few months, you'll be back by Christmas, you will.

Sergeant Carter and Sergeant Allen come to take Joey away.

Carter That's enough lad, come on…

Albert I promise we'll be together again…I swear, I swear we'll see each other again…I give you my word…

Rose hugs Albert.

All And no more will I go harvesting
Or gathering the golden corn,
For I've took the good King's shilling
And I'm off tomorrow morn.

Joey has gone, along with all the Villagers and horses. Albert confronts his father.

Albert That money's not for your bettin', or your cider

– it's for nothin' but buyin' Joey back when the war's over.

*Albert exits. **Ted** and **Rose** are alone; **Ted** feels **Rose**'s stare.*

Ted   You always said we had to sell him.

Rose   Yes. Till you said Albert could keep him.

Ted   A hundred pounds, Rose. The mortgage.

Rose   Behind his back…like a coward, Ted. You gave him your word.

Ted   We are at war Rose.

Rose   Aren't we just.

Rose walks off.

Ted   Rose…Rose…

Scene 12
Military stables, Salisbury Plain, 9 November 1914 ('Military stables scene')

*Nicholls brings in **Joey**; **Stewart**, **Topthorn**. They have just returned from manoeuvres. (Other horses are in the stables.) **Topthorn** nips **Joey** on the rear on the way in. The officers stable their horses, well apart from each other.*

Nicholls   Good boy, Joey, good boy… *[Etc.]*

Stewart   *[Simultaneously]* Topthorn…good lad… *[Etc.]*

Nicholls   They're still a bit snippy with each other!

Stewart	I think it's obvious who's top horse, don't you, Topthorn?
	The horses are stabled.
	Magnificent, isn't he?
Nicholls	Were you two far behind us in today's practice charge?
Stewart	We were marking time – Topthorn is the fastest horse in the Yeomanry.
Nicholls	Yes, I've heard you say so in the Mess, Charles.
Stewart	You have to pity those Germans on the wrong end of our charge. Our cavalry's going to cut Fritz to shreds – even your Joey will overrun them.
Nicholls	We'll flash our swords and frighten them back to Berlin, will we?
Stewart	Of course. *[To **Topthorn**]* You're ready for anything, aren't you, lad?
	*Without warning, **Stewart** fires a round from a pistol near to **Topthorn**'s head. **Topthorn** and the other horses flinch, but don't shy; **Joey** however threatens to run/shies.*
Nicholls	Charles! Easy, Joey…easy…
Stewart	Perhaps your farmboy's pony could do with some desensitising, Jamie?
	***Stewart** fires another round.*
Nicholls	For God's sake! That's enough.
	*Enter **Billy**.*
Billy	Captain Stewart.
Stewart	What is it, Narracott?

Billy	They sent me to find Major Nicholls, sir.
	Billy holds out an order, Nicholls takes it and reads. A moment.
Nicholls	*[To Stewart]* We're posted to France in the morning.
Billy	The morning?!
Stewart	*[Reprimand]* Narracott!
Billy	Sir.
Nicholls	So this is it. I trust that you're as desensitised as your horse, Captain. Tell the men to prepare. Reveille *[revally]* at five-thirty. Trooper Narracott, take Captain Stewart's horse out and into the paddock.
Billy	Sir!
	Stewart exits. Billy takes Topthorn.
Nicholls	They have to sort out which of them is in charge. Dismiss.

Scene 13
Paddock ('The fight scene')

Nicholls opens the gate. Topthorn reacts.

Nicholls	*[To Joey]* Right…do what you have to do.

Joey is unwilling to enter the paddock.

Yah!

Exit Nicholls (and Billy).

This is a big moment for Joey. We see each horse display his character in a series of challenges: cautious, exploratory, defiant.

They compete.

They seriously spar – both aggressively.
Topthorn *has the edge in speed and*
athleticism.

Dominance established, the horses are at
peace. They become friends. The hierarchy
*will be secure until **Joey**'s adaptability and*
durability make him the stronger horse during
the long years of the war.

The Bugler sounds commands.

Soldiers *load **Joey** and **Topthorn** onto:*

Scene 14
Aboard ship, 10 November 1914
('Boat/Channel crossing scene')

Joey *and **Topthorn**, uneasy at their uncertain*
*footing, fail to be comforted by **Stewart** and*
***Nicholls**.*

Sergeants Carter *and **Allan** and **Troopers***
***Billy**, **Bone** and **Greig** are on board. Other*
ships are seen in the distance.

Song reprise: ***Scarlet and the Blue***

All   Then hoorah for the Scarlet and the Blue
With the helmets a-glittering in the sun
And the bayonets flash like lightning
To the beating of a military drum
And no more will I go harvesting
Or gathering the golden corn
For I've took the good King's shilling
And I'm off tomorrow morn.

And I'll leave behind my Molly
She's the girl that I adore
And I wonder if she'll think of me

When the rifles crack and roar
And if ever I return again
And she proves true to me
We're going to do the churchyard-walk
And a sergeant's wife she'll be.

Scene 15
Quayside, Calais, France
10 November 1914 ('First Calais scene')

*The **Soldiers** disembark. **Joey** and **Topthorn** are led off the ship. **Nicholls** notices something before the others. It is wounded soldiers making their way to the ship to go home. Etched on every one of them is wretched misery and pain. There are limbs missing, bloodstains, heads that appear to be incomplete underneath bandages. Everyone is shocked by the sight of the wounded, particularly **Stewart**.*

Stewart	My God…
Nicholls	Don't show any fear or pity. This is normal, from now on.

*But **Stewart** is stunned.*

Charles…Captain Stewart!

Stewart	Sir.
Nicholls	Pull yourself together. We must rally the men. Sergeant Carter! Fall the men in!
Sergeant Carter	Sir. Troop, fall in!

*The **Soldiers** and horses fall into line.*

Nicholls	Troop! Troop-shun! To the front. Salute!

They remain until the wounded have passed.

Away. Stand at ease. Trooper Narracott, lend me your rifle.

Trooper Greig, Trooper Bone, what does this mean?

Shows rifle held horizontally, moved up and down three times.

Greig and Bone	Enemy spotted, sir!
Nicholls	Enemy indeed. We did not seek bloodshed. The German Emperor unleashed this havoc. The Kaiser's minions, his dogs of war, are responsible for those atrocities on your comrades, and they must be stopped – and you, the Yeomanry, the ordinary working men of Devon, are the men to do it: the finest soldiers in the finest army on earth! Ten miles east of here are the German infantry with very little cavalry protection. Tomorrow we will charge through them and secure the ground behind. You have each a sword, and a rifle, and one hundred and forty rounds – but what is more you have right on your side! Make the Kaiser rue the day! Let every man do himself, his King, his country, and his fallen comrades, proud! Be brave! Fear God! Honour the King!
Sergeants and Troopers	Fear God! Honour the King!

Scene 16
Open country, next day
11 November 1914 ('First charge scene')

Nicholls pans the landscape with his binoculars; the screen shows us what he sees. A Bugler appears and sounds Fall In.

Stewart   What is it, sir?

Nicholls   Enemy infantry. Open ground.

Carter   Fall in line!

Stewart   The men are ready, sir.

Nicholls gives further gestural commands. The Bugler sounds Stand By Your Horses.

Carter   Stand by your horses!

The Bugler sounds Mount.

Yeoman   Troop mount! One two three – hup!

Nicholls   Easy, Joey. Easy now, don't get excited. We'll get through this. I promise.

Everyone knows the drill. They copy when Nicholls draws his sword and rests the blade on his right shoulder.

The Bugler sounds Advance.

Troop advance!

Stewart   They're taking up positions, sir, they've seen us.

Nicholls   We keep advancing, knee to knee…

The Bugler sounds Trot.

Carter   Trot.

The horses just begin to move – the Bugler sounds Gallop.

Gallop!

Nicholls	Charge!

The Bugler sounds Charge.

Carter	Charge!

Incoming enemy machine gun fire.

Nicholls	My God! What the hell is that? Machine guns?! Attacking right flank! Break line! Fall back!

Stewart	Break the line! Fall back! Fall back! Machine gun!

Incoming artillery rounds.

*Suddenly, **Nicholls** flies off **Joey**'s back. Freeze. **Joey**'s confused.*

Chaos.

***Nicholls** is hurled through the air. Unfreeze.*

*Before they've got going, horses and riders begin to fall. **Stewart** and **Topthorn** find **Joey**.*

Stewart	Hi-yah!

***Stewart** reaches across to grab **Joey**'s reins.*

Whoa! Break the line! Fall back! Machine gun! Right flank! Machine gun! Fall back! Fall back! Machine gun! Fall back! Fall back!

*Enter **Song Woman** (not Song Man) and **Women of the Village**.*

Song: ***Devonshire Carol***

Song Woman	The lambkin in the manger The light upon the lea The moorland yields to glory The shepherds bend the knee —

Women of the Village	And all are wrapped in grace And all are gifted mirth Peace walks upon this blessèd land Goodwill upon all earth.

*The **Women** kneel at their dead as:*

Scene 17
Ted and Rose's farm, Christmas Day, 1914. ('Christmas scene')

*Enter **Ted**, pushing a second-hand bicycle with a ribbon tied to it. Enter **Rose** from the house, leading **Albert**, hands over his eyes.*

Rose	You can look, now. Happy Christmas, Albert.
Albert	*[To **Rose**]* …A bicycle. Thanks.
Rose	Father fixed it up.
Albert	*[To **Rose**]* It's grand. I'll ride it.
Rose	Well, that's what it's for, Albert: to sit on and ride. You know the Christmas present I'd like? You two to talk.

*Enter **Arthur**.*

Oh…Arthur…!

Arthur	Yes, um. I was down at the post office, last night, just before closin', and while I was there, Mrs Allan said there was a parcel for Albert, from the, from the, from over there, and I thought, I could go up that way in the morning, so…
Rose	Thank you, Arthur.
Albert	Who's sending me a parcel from over there?
Rose	Open it and see. Happy Christmas, Arthur.

Albert   Happy Christmas, Uncle Arthur.

Arthur   Oh, um. Happy Christmas.

Rose   What is it?

Albert   I don't know…a book, or…

Rose   There's your name.

Albert   My name?… It's drawings…a sketchbook…?
[Gasp of realisation] Look! It's a picture of me
and Joey! It must be from Major Nicholls!

Rose   Well I never. You and Joey?

Albert   Look! Look – he sees him beautiful!

Rose   There's a letter.

Albert hands it to Rose to read.

"Dear Albert Narracott, Major James
Nicholls…Major James Nicholls who died in
action today, left you this. Yours, acting Major
Charles Stewart."

Arthur   Erm, I wouldn't have brought it if I'd have
known – Well, I'll…

Arthur makes to leave.

Rose   Arthur! Have you heard from Billy?

Arthur   Yes. Um, not for a while…There's been some
telegrams received yesterday…informing. You
know…Thomas Bone, John Greig, Auctioneer
Carter; Christmas Eve…terrible.

Ted   Papers say it's going according to plan —

Arthur   Yes, Yes. That's right, they got the whole
British Empire there…Australians, Canadians,
Indians, Africans…maybe our village has been
unlucky. I'm right behind our boys.

Ted	So am I. Billy'll be back.
Rose	Oh, he will, he will.
Arthur	It's just all this barbed wire we've been hearin' about; horses won't see that, they'll run straight into it. And in my day they didn't have these machine guns.
Ted	In your day?
Arthur	That's right, Ted. In my day, when I fought for the Empire.
Rose	Come in to the house for a cup of tea, Arthur. We were just about to have one.
Ted	Were we?

*Exit **Ted**. Exit **Arthur**.*

Rose	You bliddin' men…
Albert	He was ridin' Joey.
Rose	Whatcha say?
Albert	Major Nicholls he was ridin' Joey when he died.
Rose	You don't know that.
Albert	"In action", you said!
Rose	We'll have to wait and see —
Albert	He promised he'd look after 'im!
Rose	Can ye just shut up about yer bliddin' horse, half the men in the village are dead!

*A moment. **Rose** envelops **Albert** in her arms.*

I don't know what to be sayin'…he might be all right. I've a little something for you…

***Rose** makes to leave.*

Albert	Mother.
Rose	Yes, son?
Albert	I do like my bicycle.
Rose	I know he done it all the wrong way, Albert. I think he knows it too.

*Exit **Rose**.*

Albert	Well then, Albert…come on, then.

__Albert__ tears a __Joey__ picture out of the sketchbook. Exit __Albert__, on his bicycle.

Come on then Albert!

*Enter **Rose**, with a present.*

Rose	It's only a silly little something —

__Rose__ finds the sketchbook with the page torn out.

Albert? Albert? Albert! Albert! Ted! He's gone! Albert! Albert!

Scene 18
Behind British lines,
beginning of March 1915
('Second charge scene')

The Bugler sounds Fall In.

__Joey__, __Topthorn__ and a shell-shocked __Billy__. Enter __Stewart__.

Stewart	Narracott?

Distant explosion.

Billy	S-s-s-sir?
Stewart	You're riding Joey in this charge.

Billy   J-J-J-Joey? He's m-m-mine?

A barrage starts up, startling the horses.

Stewart   Stop shaking. You'll unsettle the horses. Have a tot of rum.

Stewart hands Billy his hip-flask. Distant explosion. Billy drops the hip-flask.

Billy   Sorry, sir —

Stewart   That's our guns destroying their barbed wire defences. Do you hear me?

Billy   S-s-sir, what about their m-m-m-machine guns? Sir?

Distant explosion.

Stewart   [Ignores this] That's our guns shelling their barbed wire so we can get through. Joey will look after you, Narracott.

Huge explosion; Billy terrified.

Billy   N-n-n-no…he w-won't…

Stewart   Trooper, pull yourself together!

Billy   I mean the horse is just the horse, sir. It's m-my f-f-father and my grandf-f-father who will be guiding my hand, sir.

Stewart   That's the spirit. [Re. Joey] Back him up, back him up!

Billy obeys.

The Bugler sounds Stand By Your Horses.

When we charge, head for the gaps in the barbed wire and give them cold steel.

The Bugler sounds Mount.

One, two, three, hup!

*They mount. Huge explosions. **Topthorn** is agitated.*

Easy, Topthorn. Good lad.

Billy It's all right, Joey boy. It's all right.

The Bugler sounds Advance.

Sergeant *[Off]* Troop advance!

Billy I can't see any gaps. The barbed wire it's everywhere, sir.

***Stewart** draws his sword. **Billy** copies him. The Bugler sounds Trot.*

Sergeant Trot!

Billy Where are the gaps?! Where are the gaps?!

***Stewart** makes the Commanding Officer's signal – sword vertical held high – the Bugler sounds Charge.*

*After **Stewart**'s example the men sweep their swords down to point at the enemy.*

Stewart Chaaaarrgge!

Sergeant Charge!

For a few moments horses gallop freely, then the enemy guns start up. The men use their battle cries to whip themselves into a frenzy.

Incoming shells and machine gunfire create havoc. The ground erupts.

Billy There aren't any gaps!

***Joey** and **Topthorn** keep going.*

Stewart We have to jump the wire! Jump the barbed wire! Jump the bloody wire!

*Obeying, **Joey** and **Topthorn** leap. Blackout. House lights up.*

Topthorn, Captain Stewart, Joey and Billy

Topthorn and Joey

Act 2

Scene 1
Quayside, Calais, beginning of March 1915 ('Second Calais scene')

*Enter **Song Man** playing the harmonica.*

*Enter infantry privates, including **David Taylor**. Enter **Albert**, in Yeomanry uniform. He is adrift.*

*Enter **Sergeant Thunder**.*

Sergeant Thunder	*Bonjour, mes amis!* Spring is in the air. Shame you're not on your Grand Tour of Europe. Nice is very nice this time of year, I'm told. But you're not headed there, and neither am I, more's the pity. Platoon, fall in! Platoon 'shun!

Infantry obey.

Oi, you! Name?

Albert	Trooper Albert Narracott, Sergeant.
Sergeant Thunder	"Trooper" Narracott…

***Sergeant Thunder** finds him on list.*

Ah yes. New orders. You're joining the infantry.

Albert	Sir?
Sergeant Thunder	Don't call me sir I'm not an effing officer I work for a living! Hang about; how old are you?
Albert	Nineteen, Sergeant.

***Sergeant Thunder** stares at **Albert**. **Albert** doesn't wilt.*

Sergeant Thunder	More like sixteen…You've been effing transferred, Private Narracott, because the Yeomanry mob you were to join doesn't exist any more.
Albert	Don't exist?
Sergeant Thunder	Correct.
Albert	What about Billy Narracott, 'e's my cousin, 'e's with that Yeomanry.
Sergeant Thunder	Any survivors will have been absorbed into —
Albert	What about the horses? My horse went with them, 'e's called Joey, this is his picture, see.
Sergeant Thunder	You have a picture of your horse? Why didn't you say? Ah yes, a simple sketch but unmistakably – what did you say his name was?
Albert	Joey.
Sergeant Thunder	— I don't know where your effing Joey is! Do I look like I know the latest on every effing horse in the war? Do I look like an effing equine expert or even an effing equestrian enthusiast?!
Albert	But you said there were survivors —
Sergeant Thunder	Silence, Private!…Are you silent, now?
Albert	Sergeant!
Sergeant Thunder	You spoke!
Albert	Sergeant!
Sergeant Thunder	You spoke again!
	David is caught containing laughter.
Sergeant Thunder	You! Here! Now! And what, pray, is your name?
David	Private Taylor, Sergeant.
Sergeant Thunder	This one here thinks he's on a mission for the

	Prevention of Cruelty to Animals, he thinks he's come to comb the fields of France for his pony, but you know the real reason we're here, don't you, Private Taylor?
David	To win the war, Sergeant.
Sergeant Thunder	That's right: we've come to France to kill Germans. Either of you know any French? Never mind. I'll learn you some. Repeat after me. Je suis un bloody sod.
David and Albert	Je suis un bloody sod.
Sergeant Thunder	Je suis un bloody idiot.
David and Albert	Je suis un bloody idiot.
Sergeant Thunder	Right, now, I want you all to come and pick up a shovel from over here. You think I'm joking? Move it. I said move it, move it, move it! Six months we've been here and it could be another six before we go home – so we are going to burrow deep into those fields and make ourselves cosy in the clay! That's right boys, trenches, the deeper you burrow, the cosier you is. Platoon! Platoon 'shun! Right turn, toot sweet to the Front; and the tooter the sweeter! Platoon, by the left, quick march.

Song: ***Dolly Gray***

Song Man	Goodbye, Dolly, I must leave you —

Singing as they exit.

All	Though it breaks my heart to go
Something tells me I am needed
At the front to fight the foe…

See the soldier boys are marching
And I can no longer stay… |

Scene 2
A farm in the Somme Valley, beginning of March 1915 ('First Paulette scene')

Screen shows horses trapped on the wire.

*German soldiers have occupied the farm. Many are wounded. They are being seen to by **Dr Schweyk** and **Private Schnabel**, an ambulance orderly.*

*Enter **Paulette** a Frenchwoman, the owner of the farm, and **Emilie** her daughter.*

Paulette	What are you doing? This is my farm!
Schnabel	I don't speak French. We need this land as a casualty clearing station. We're requisitioning it.

Schnabel goes about his business. Paulette shouts after him.

Paulette	You can't do this here!

*Enter **Billy** and **Stewart**, POWs under German guard (one of the soldiers is **Brandt**). **Billy** is very distressed.*

Billy	What are they going to do with us, sir?
Stewart	Keep quiet, Narracott.
Paulette	What are you doing to them? This is my land not a German prison!

*Enter **Private Klausen** and **Captain Friedrich Müller**. **Friedrich** has horse blood on his hands and uniform; **Klausen** has a gash on his face. **Friedrich** goes over to **Stewart** and **Billy**. **Klausen** follows.*

Friedrich	Major.
Stewart	Captain.
Friedrich	That British charge was madness.
Stewart	I don't speak German.
Friedrich	Fifteen horses were caught in the barbed wire – I had to shoot fifteen of them.
Klausen	If only they were British soldiers.
Friedrich	The whole thing is a fiasco. To ride straight into barbed wire and machine guns? – barbaric.
Stewart	I don't speak German, Fritz.
Klausen	What did he say?
Friedrich	I don't know. Perhaps he insulted us?
Klausen	You filthy Tommy idiot —
Friedrich	Easy —
Billy	Sir, what are they saying?
Friedrich	[To **Stewart**] My orderly is jumpy, Major. All his comrades, killed or wounded by your British shells.
Stewart	I don't understand a damn word you're saying.
Billy	Sir –? They're gonna kill us, ain't they?
Friedrich	Search them!
	Very agitated, **Billy** *has his hand to his pocket.*
	What's he got there?
Billy	No…no!
Stewart	Trooper!
Billy	It's my father's!

Stewart	What is?
Soldier (Brandt)	He's armed!
	*They aim at **Billy**. He has **Arthur**'s knife in his hand.*
Klausen	I'll shoot, I'll shoot —
Billy	I don't understand them —
Klausen	Drop it or I'll shoot, drop it!
Stewart	Give it to them!
Billy	No! It's my father's!
Stewart	Narracott…!
	*Klausen shoots **Billy** dead.*
	Billy…
Friedrich	Klausen.
Stewart	You didn't have to do that —
	*Klausen takes **Billy**'s knife and turns on **Stewart**.*
Friedrich	Private!
Klausen	I'll slash you to pieces with it!
Stewart	I'm unarmed! I'm unarmed!
Friedrich	Private, that's enough!
Klausen	Captain.
	*Enter **Joey** and **Topthorn**, in great distress, led by **German soldiers** who can't handle them: **Topthorn** is a particular problem. **Friedrich** is taken with them. **Stewart** tries to calm **Topthorn**; **Brandt** allows it, gun still on **Stewart**, as the horses are dangerous.*

Stewart	Topthorn…Topthorn…Easy!
Friedrich	These are the two magnificent horses that managed to jump the barbed wire; you owe them your life, Major.
Stewart	Easy, Topthorn…
Friedrich	Topthorn? *[Re. **Stewart**]* Brandt, take the Major to Colonel Strauss. Don't harm him, that's an order.
Brandt	Captain.
Stewart	Goodbye, Topthorn. Goodbye, Old Lad.
Friedrich	Klausen, get me some water.

*Exit **Stewart**, under **Brandt**'s guard.*

***Friedrich** expertly calms **Topthorn**. He "joins up" with him, just as **Albert** inadvertently did with **Baby Joey** – but **Friedrich** knows what he is doing.*

*Exit **Dr Schweyk**.*

	Shhh, calm down. Calm down, my friend. Calm down, Topthorn. Friedrich will look after you.

*With water, **Friedrich** sees to the wound.*

Klausen	To them you are Friedrich, to us you are —
Friedrich	*[To **Klausen**, re. **Billy**]* Take away that body. Then get that gash seen to, and Klausen, pull yourself together.
Klausen	Captain.

*As **Friedrich** tends to the horses, he opens up to them. **Klausen** notices this; then he and another soldier take **Billy**'s body away.*

Friedrich	I know, Topthorn. I know what you've seen. My horse got it yesterday. Shrapnel through the brain…I know. Easy…That will heal. You are a magnificent horse, but now you join the German cavalry. You simply turn around and face the English machine guns with me.

*Re-enter **Dr Schweyk**, with **Colonel Strauss**.*

Strauss	*Schnabel!* Schnabel! The Frenchwoman's cart will make an ambulance, harness the horses to it and drive the wounded to base hospital.
Friedrich	But, Colonel, those horses can't pull, they're a thoroughbred and a hunter.
Strauss	We don't have a choice, Captain Müller!
Friedrich	But, Colonel —
Strauss	Do it!
Strauss	Schnabel, put red crosses on the cart.
Friedrich	Colonel.

*Exit **Strauss**.*

Friedrich	*[Laughs]* What did I tell you? – No one even knows the difference between a cavalry horse and a cart-horse –
	Still…if you can do it…you won't have to ride into British guns tomorrow…

***Friedrich** tries to persuade **Topthorn** to take a collar…*

You've probably never seen one of these, let alone worn it…but if you could, you'd get to stay behind the lines, out of the gunfire… easy…it'd save your life, Topthorn…easy, boy…come on, Topthorn, come on…

…But he fails…

Dr Schweyk	Captain Müller?
Friedrich	It's impossible, Dr Schweyk, you might as well hitch me to the cart!
Dr Schweyk	I will if that's the only way to stop these men from bleeding to death.
Friedrich	*[To **Topthorn**, urgent]* Where do you want to be – safe here, pulling an ambulance, or out there, snarled and dying in the wire?

*Friedrich makes another attempt to collar **Topthorn** – the rejection is emphatic. At which point, **Joey** volunteers for the collar.*

*Enter **Song Man**.*

Song: **Plough Song**

Song Man	The ploughboy's written home a letter The best that he knew how — Saying this cruel war shall ne'er keep us apart —
Friedrich	What?
Song Man	While canon loud do roar I shall keep our love secure —
Friedrich	You have done this before?
Song Man	For my tunic buttons tight around your heart.
Dr Schweyk	There. Not so hard.
Friedrich	To use a beautiful hunter like you as a cart-horse! So it's the British who are madmen! Why do you know how to take a collar?! What is your name?
Schnabel	I heard that Tommy called him "Joey, Joey".

Dr Schweyk	*[Instructing **Schnabel** to help him with another wounded soldier to put on the cart]* Schnabel!
Schnabel	Yes, Dr Schweyk…
Friedrich	Joey…whoever taught you just saved your life. Yeah? Come on, Topthorn…do what Joey did…

Topthorn smells Joey's harness, then smells his own, etc.

…Nothing to be frightened of…that's right, good lad…good lad…

Topthorn is harnessed. He remains anxious about the harness and cart. Joey's calmness encourages Topthorn.

Well done, boys. You're out of the fighting – for now. Play your cards right, this could see you through the war. And I'm with you, till tomorrow. After that, who knows? Who knows anything…

Explosions start in the distance.

*With the wounded bodies on the cart, **Friedrich** urges **Joey** and **Topthorn** towards the hospital.*

Joey leads the way. Screen pans to another part of France.

Scene 3
A shallow crater in disputed territory, that night, March 1915 ('Crater scene')

Following a successful, surprise German attack.
Albert *dives in, closely followed by **David**.*

Overhead shelling throughout scene.

Albert   Fritz your way?

David   No. Yours?

David Taylor and Albert

Albert   No. We're right in it.

David   Where did they come from?

Albert   First I knew, they were in our trench. The only English I heard was "Fall back! Fall back!"

David   So what should we do now?

Albert   Why are you asking me?

David   I followed you 'cause I thought you knew what you were doing.

Albert   I was scared stupid, Private. Scared stupid.

David   Are we the only ones who made it?

Albert   Can't be.

David   Might be.

Albert   Can't be.

David   Shall we make a run for it?

Albert   But we're lost so which way?

David   …Dunno.

Albert   We could be running towards them.

David   Come on, Albert, you're the country boy, you're the one who buggers about in fields at night.

Albert   Nothin' to see is there? Nothin'. No stars, no moon…

David   Nothing. Oh no, we're buggered ain't we?

Albert   No, no. We can't be the only ones who made it.

David   …I'm gonna finish a letter to my girl —

Albert   — Now?

David Will you —

Albert Yes —

David See it gets —

Albert Yes —

David If anything happens to —

Albert Shut up! Nothing's going to happen.

David writes. Albert alone hears something: a horse screaming.

David What is it?

Albert Nothing.

They listen. They look. Nothing. Albert stares at his picture of Joey.

David You gonna write a letter to your horse?

Albert *Très* funny.

David Well, Can he read?…Your silence reveals that the answer to my question is neeeeeigh.

Albert Is that your girl's picture?

David Yeah that's her. That's my Flossie.

Albert At least Joey's meant to look like a horse.

David If Flossie's got a long face it's because she's missing me giving her a rub down after a gallop. She's what keeps me going…When I was climbing out of our trench I put my foot through something. I think it was a bit of a man, Albert.

Albert It might well have been, Private. Forget it.

David And I've got a little brother, Alfie. Promised I'd teach him to ride a bicycle.

Albert   Has he got one?

David   No.

Albert   I've a spare bicycle. I left it in Exeter. If it's still there Alfie can have it.

David   Thanks, Albert. That's *bon*.

Albert   'S all right.

David   Albert…I could help you write a letter, you know…if you can't.

Albert   I can. I just don't have no one to write to.

Albert alone hears another horse scream.

What was that?

David   What was what?

Albert   That…

David   What?

Albert   Joey!

David   Albert?

Albert   I will find Joey, David. I will. I know he's somewhere in this mess and I know he's alive.

David   Whatever keeps you going. I've got me girl. You've got your horse.

A German soldier falls into their crater, or approaches it.

German Soldier   Here! Here!

Albert   Is that Fritz? Christ!

Albert shoots the German before the German shoots him.

Jesus!

David	Now we're for it.

They come under attack. It starts a battle.

Albert	That way!
David	Reckon?
Albert	Whadda you think?
David	I think so…

*Exit **Albert** and **David**. Screen pans back to:*

Scene 4
Paulette's farm in the Somme Valley, the following morning, March 1915 ('Second Paulette Scene')

***Schnabel** enters to move the plough.*
***Dr Schweyk** comes running in and yells.*

Dr Schweyk	Run! Run! Run!

*There is an explosion and both men are killed. Crows enter. **Emilie** opens the door and sees the crows right away.*

***Emilie** exits the house to deal with the crows who peck at the bodies of two dead German soldiers, **Schnabel** and **Dr Schweyk**.*

Emilie	Shoo! Shoo!

***Emilie** can't help but look at the dead bodies. She inspects them. Are they alive?*

Hello?

Then on one of them she discovers…

Chocolate!

*Friedrich enters with **Topthorn** and **Joey***.

Friedrich Hello?…

*Hearing **Friedrich**, **Emilie** hides behind a plough.*

***Joey**, **Topthorn** and **Friedrich** are completing a trip from the hospital. **Friedrich** is still in his cavalry uniform but it's battered and bloody. **Topthorn** is still inconvenienced by his wound.*

…Hello, Dr Schweyk, we're back, they managed it, you can promote me back to captain —

***Friedrich** sees the dead.*

He recognises a body.

Schnabel…

And another body.

Dr Schweyk. Dead —

***Joey** has discovered **Emilie**. **Friedrich** becomes aware of movement, takes out his gun, and shoots at the plough. **Emilie** screams, another crow flies away. She is terrified. They misunderstand each other.*

Oh, God. It's all right, it's all right, I'm not going to harm you! See…

***Friedrich** puts the gun down.*

…It's all right…

***Friedrich** is struck by how similar she looks to his daughter.*

Why are you alone? Where is your mother?

***Friedrich** knows she can't understand him, and uses gestures as much as words.*

My name is Friedrich. What is yours? I won't hurt you. Friedrich. Here…

*Friedrich takes out a photograph, compares it with **Emilie**, tries to make her understand.*

…My daughter…Gisa.

*Emilie is calmer now. She watches **Joey**.*

Won't you please tell me your name? Friedrich. You?

*Now **Friedrich** understands that **Joey** is the way to communicate with her.*

Joey. Joey.

Emilie	Joey? Emilie.
Friedrich	Ah, Emilie. Say bonjour to Emilie, Topthorn.
Emilie	Topzorn?
Friedrich	Top*th*orn.
Emilie	Topzorn.

*Emilie lavishes attention on **Joey**. He eats her chocolate, though she offered it to **Topthorn**.*

Joey! Joey!

Friedrich	She likes you, Joey.
Emilie	Naughty boy, Joey…

*Emilie pets **Joey**. (Though both horses become restless – they are thirsty.)*

They're thirsty!

Friedrich	What?

*Emilie rushes towards some buckets with water. They are too heavy for her to lift, so **Friedrich** helps.*

Ah, I see! You are a farmer's daughter!

Joey and Topthorn drink from the buckets
Emilie brushes Joey.

Friedrich [Pointing at the photo again] My Gisa is already eleven. That's my wife. [Points to photograph] My daughter. And that – who's that? That's me! You see, Emilie…this war is meant to make men, but I'm half the man I was.

Emilie sings Lullee Lullay (in French).
She becomes his daughter, Gisa. We go
somewhere else.

Gisa? Gisa? I don't know who I am anymore Topthorn…dead behind the eyes…an unfeeling murderer…who could kill a child… if only I could somehow alter my fate…not be who they bred me to be.

An idea occurs to him and suddenly his pace changes with the thrill of the idea.

Yes. Oh, yes, that's clever thinking, Joey –
– A new uniform…become someone else. Not be Cavalry-Captain Friedrich Müller at all…

Friedrich takes the dead private's uniform.

…But ambulance orderly Johann Schnabel. I know, if they find me out, it's the firing squad, but I would be out of the cavalry and safe behind the lines, as you are…stay here at the clearing station, look after you…till after the fighting.

Friedrich pulls the uniform half on. Emilie is by now regarding him.

What is it? What are you looking at? Gisa… Gisa?

Emilie	Emilie.
Friedrich	Emilie, you must understand, my child, the cavalry has no place in this war! The machine guns are laughing at us, Emilie. Look at Joey – do you think he deserves to die out there? The Kaiser will win or lose without me, and if they think me no better than a deserter, well then Topthorn, I never deserted you.

Friedrich finishes putting on the uniform, adding his red cross arm bands and hat.

Emilie	F-F-Friedrich?
Friedrich	Yes. You can still call me Friedrich.

*Enter **Paulette**. Dialogue overlaps:*

Paulette	Emilie! Emilie!
Emilie	Mama!
Paulette	Why aren't you in the cellar?
Friedrich	Madame, please don't be alarmed…friend…
Paulette	I told you, never speak to Germans!
Friedrich	No, friend…
Paulette	Indoors at once!
Emilie	But, Mama, the horses need me!
Paulette	Go!
Friedrich	Please, Madame —
Emilie	It's not fair!
Friedrich	Please don't take her!

*Emilie has gone, and **Paulette** blocks **Friedrich** from the house. **Friedrich** is on his own, and suddenly the plan seems like madness:*

God, what am I doing?

*Before **Friedrich** can take off the private's uniform **Sergeant Klebb** enters, and he has to commit to the disguise.*

Klebb	Private? Private!
Friedrich	Yes, Sergeant!
Klebb	Where's Dr Schweyk?
Friedrich	Dead, Sergeant.
Klebb	You're the only orderly?
Friedrich	Yes, Sergeant.
Klebb	Any sign of Cavalry-Captain Friedrich Müller?
Friedrich	Captain Friedrich Müller? Dead.

Scene starts to change over the next line…

Klebb   Bury them. We need to expand the clearing station – be ready for more wounded. Stretcher here!

*Exit **Klebb**.*

Friedrich   Dead, Topthorn. But now you and I will lug this ambulance back and forth together. Back and forth along the banks of the River Somme, till Kaisers and kings come to their senses. And then I promise I'll take you home…home to little Gisa…

Scene 5
A trench / Ted and Rose's farm / Paulette's farm, 30 June, and some time in September, 1916 ('Triptych scene')

*Enter **Song Man** and **Song Woman**.*

Song: ***Snowfalls and Stand To Reprise***

*In the trench, **Albert** is dictating a letter – his first, and perhaps last – to **David**. Other men are in the trench. Suppressed anticipation, tension.*

*At Ted and Rose's farm, **Rose** enters to find **Ted**, calling his name. She is holding a letter, barely able to control her emotions.*

*At Paulette's farm, **Friedrich** drags bodies into the gloom.*

Song Man	Cruel winter cuts through like the reaper —
Rose	Ted…Ted…
Song Man	The old year lies withered and slain
Rose	Ted.
Song Man	And like Barleycorn who rose from the grave A new year will rise up again.

Music continues.

Albert	I've found a chum called David.
David	*[Writes]* "I've found a good chum called David."
Albert	And they've promoted me to Colonel.
David	*Très* funny.
Albert	I'm in northern France, near the Somme river, and horse in French is "cheval".

David	Bloody hell, Albert, how am I gonna spell that?
Ted	Does it have a date?
Rose	It says the 30th of June, 1916 – anything could've happened to him since then!
Ted	Read.
Rose	"Dear Mother. I am all right. I've found a good chum called David, he's very handsome, and he's writing this letter for me. And they've promoted me to lance-corporal…" Then they've blacked something out…I wonder what he wrote there?
Ted	Go on.
Rose	"Horse in French is shovel."
Albert	Ju shursh Joey means I look for Joey.
Rose	"Ju shursh Joey means I look for — " he's still looking for that horse!

Arthur has appeared. Music out.

Arthur?

Arthur	Mornin'…I, er…
Rose	Oh, Arthur, we been worried, nobody in the village has seen you.
Arthur	I, um…Mrs Allan came and told me you received a letter.

Rose nods, looks to Ted, glances through letter, shakes her head.

Rose	I'm sorry. Albert don't mention Billy.

Arthur has his eyes to the ground, and now perhaps suppresses his grief with a choke.

Ted	Is there anything else in the letter?

Albert	And put this, if you can spell it. You're a *bon* mother.
Rose	"You're a *bon* mother." *Bon*.
Ted	Nothin' else?

Snowfalls underscore resumes.

*Rose reads for a second, then shakes her head. A moment of rapprochement between the brothers, until **Arthur** goes his way, **Ted** his. **Rose** looks after them, then returns to the letter.*

*At Paulette's, enter **Emilie** and **Friedrich**, followed by **Paulette** with a garland of flowers.*

Albert	Don't read this part to Father. He was wrong, Mother, and I won't stop till I've got Joey back, so don't be angry with me for running away. Don't worry, we're in farmland here. It could almost be home.
Emilie	*[Giggling]* No, no, Friedrich, your French is terrible! Repeat after me, listen properly. Whatever happens —
Friedrich	Whatever happens…
Emilie	We will always take —
Friedrich	We will always take…
Emilie	Joey and Topzorn —
Friedrich	Joey and Topzorn…
Emilie	Away from danger!
Friedrich	Away from danger.
Emilie	Very good, Friedrich! Let's shake hands!

Emilie holds out her hand, a brisk handshake.
Paulette gives Friedrich the garland; he
places it on Emilie's head.

Song Man	I will garland a bonnet of daisies — To crown you the Queen of the May —
Paulette	There.
Friedrich	Like a princess.
Song Man	And all shall behold —
Emilie	On Joey!
Song Man	— the seasons unfold As surely as night follows day —

Friedrich, Paulette, Emilie, Topthorn and Joey

Friedrich helps *Emilie* mount *Joey*.

Song Woman	Phoebe arise, a gleam in her eyes,
	And the year turns round again —
Friedrich	That's what he was born for!
Song Man	And like Barleycorn who rose from the grave…
David	Did you want me to say your loving son?

Albert nods.

Friedrich exits to see to more wounded. *Paulette* goes indoors. *Emilie* continues to ride *Joey*, and even falls asleep on him.

Rose	"Albert."
David	Why didn't you tell her about over the top? Or the trench foot, or the bloody whizz-bangs, and the rats and – Jesus, it's this waiting I can't stand, if we're going, let's get out of this ditch and go!
Albert	That's right, Private, when they blow the whistle, we just do it, right?
David	Charge and fire; glory or the end, eh?! Or a Blighty wound? Some shrapnel in the leg – just enough to get us home.
Albert	We'll get behind that bloody Jerry line, but we ain't going home.
David	'Cause your Joey's gonna be over there in that pretty French farmland, is he?
Albert	Maybe he bloody is.
Song Man	Stand to, me bonnie lads —
Albert	Stand-to.
Song Man	May angels now attend thee —

Rose   Ted?

*Rose pursues **Ted**.*

Song Man   Be steadfast, bonnie lads —

Albert   When we go, we walk, right?

Song Man   From earthly dread defend thee —

Albert   Slow pace.

David   Jesus, Jesus, Jesus…

Song Man   One final hurried prayer —

Albert   Keep in a straight line, don't bunch up —

Song Man   A whistle rakes the air —

David   What if I want to run?

Song Man   Stand to, me bonnie lads —

Albert   Orders, David: walk!

Song Man   Hold the line right steady.

Albert   We'll get to their trenches.

Distant explosions.

That's the big push started.

David   Oh, God.

Albert   Joey. Joey. Joey.

David   *[Overlapping]* Oh, God, oh, God, oh, God, oh, God, oh, God.

*(Optional: the verbalised countdown, 10 to 1, to go over the top begins. Place this rhythmically against the remainder of the scene at **Paulette**'s.) (The actors playing **Albert** and **David** disappear here to get into position for the next scene.)*

Emilie wakes.

Emilie Good boy, Joey…good boy…

Suddenly the thunder of shelling is very close. *Joey* and *Topthorn* are distressed. *Paulette* *rushes from the house with a bag full of* *belongings.*

Paulette Emilie? Emilie!

Emilie Mama…

Paulette My God…Emilie!

Enter **Friedrich**.

Friedrich I need the horses…for the ambulance…I need them!

Paulette No. No! We need them!

Friedrich There are more wounded.

Paulette Come with us away from here.

Friedrich What?

Paulette Help us to get away, German. To go, leave.

Friedrich I can't just desert.

Paulette I'm not staying here to watch my daughter die.

Emilie Friedrich, whatever happens we must always take Joey and Topzorn away from danger.

Shelling, louder: Paulette's house is in ruins. *The horses show distress.*

Paulette My God no!

Friedrich [To **Paulette**] Madame…we can't stay here…

Paulette Where can we go?

Friedrich Anywhere…Away…East.

Paulette   Yes, we go east.

Friedrich, Paulette, Emilie and the horses disappear (as the countdown has reached "One") as the officer's whistle blows ear-piercingly and:

Scene 6
Over the top, July 1916
('Over the top scene')

Silence. Nothingness.

Soldiers advance. David and Albert and others. And more on the screen.

David   Albert…

Albert   It's all right, David…

David   Albert…

Albert   Walk. Slowly. That stinkhole trench seems like heaven now, eh?

David   We're not gonna make it through this.

Soldiers

Albert	Yes we are. Glory, right? Do it for Flossie.
David	Flossie, yeah.
Albert	Flossie with the long face…
David	Not as long as your Joey's.
Albert	That's it, good boy.

Gunfire starts up in the distance.

Goodbye, Dolly, I must leave you…

Soldiers down the line join in the song one by one.

Soldiers	Though it breaks my heart to go —
Albert	Sing out, lads!
Albert and Soldiers	Something tells me I am needed At the front to fight the foe…

Bombardment begins. Explosions on screen. Men fall one by one. But not Albert and David.

See the soldier boys are marching
And I can no longer stay
Hark, I hear the bugle calling —

A huge explosion.

Any remaining men fall.

Albert and David are caught in a nightmare. Then David also falls and Albert is alone!

A strange soundscape, like tinnitus: we are in their terror. Albert is witness to the horror around him.

Albert discovers David lying on the ground.

Albert	David? Lads? David? Wake up David, David. Wake Up…

Gunfire. The geography widens – an obliterated landscape becomes apparent as:

***Albert**, still walking, faces the devastation, and…*

Screen goes from men and explosions to huge bleeding poppies and…

*Now **Albert** is resolved to fight, heading for the German trenches:*

Albert   I'll get you, Fritz. I'll smash you, Fritz, I'll smash you…you bloody idiots, I'll cut you down, you're done for…I'll massacre you…You killed David! David!!!

Paulette   *[Off]* I've told you a thousand times, Emilie, we'll be safe there, now keep up!

Albert   David…

***Albert** disappears: God knows what his fate is. The poppies fall away as:*

Scene 7
A country road against the obliterated landscape, July 1916 ('Gun team scene')

The dead remain.

*Enter **Friedrich** with a map and binoculars, leading **Paulette** riding **Topthorn**.*

Paulette   I've told you a thousand times, Emilie, we'll be safe there, now keep up!

Emilie   *[As **Emilie** rides in on **Joey**]* And there'll be no soldiers there, it'll be just us and Joey and Topthorn?

Paulette   Yes, Emilie, yes!

Joey and *Topthorn* *sense the arrival of horses of death and* *Friedrich* *stops, alert.*

Friedrich   Quiet. Wait.

Friedrich *looks through binoculars and spots approaching German platoon.*

Friedrich *signals to* *Paulette*, *she gets down off* *Topthorn*.

Klausen   *[Off]* Pull! Pull! Pull! Pull! Come on, you beasts. Pull!

Paulette   Emilie!

Friedrich, *Paulette*, *Topthorn*, *and* *Emilie* *riding* *Joey* *escape (off stage).*

Emilie!

Enter *Klausen* *(rank now Lance-Corporal) and German soldiers (*Franz* and* *Jurgen*) pulling two knackered horses –* *Heine* *and* *Coco* *– pulling an artillery piece. The horses are being lashed.*

Klausen   *[To gun team]* Halt!

Klausen *spots* *Friedrich* *and calls after him.*

— Private! Private! *[To the* **German Soldiers***]* Stop them!

The **German Soldiers** *run off and bring back* **Friedrich**, **Emilie**, **Paulette**, **Joey** *and* **Topthorn**. **Friedrich** *conceals himself, pulls down his hat.*

Friedrich   Yes, Lance-Corporal.

Klausen   Are you taking these women somewhere?

Friedrich   Yes, Lance-Corporal. To Rancourt. This woman's farm was decimated.

Klausen	I need your horses for this field gun. We're repositioning it.
Friedrich	But, Lance-Corporal —
Klausen	What? *[To the **German Soldiers**]* Harness them.

*The **German Soldiers** approach **Joey** and **Topthorn**. **Franz** starts to move **Joey** towards the gun.*

Emilie	What are they doing – ? Friedrich!
Paulette	Emilie, ssshh.
Klausen	What did she call you? Take your hat off. Take it off!

*Friedrich does so. **Klausen** recognises him.*

Captain Müller? You? *[To the **German Soldiers**]* I know this man! He's no orderly, he was my captain. You were deserting? With them – and these horses? Hitch them to the gun, you filthy coward!

*Klausen spits at **Friedrich**.*

Emilie	Friedrich! Friedrich!
Paulette	No! Emilie!

*Klausen takes out his gun and aims it at **Paulette** and **Emilie**.*

Klausen	Leave right now, or I'll shoot!
Friedrich	Paulette, go back, back, I'm sorry...
Emilie	Joey...
Klausen	Go!
Friedrich	I'll look after him, Emilie, I promise...
Paulette	Emilie...

Paulette pulls Emilie off against her will.

Emilie No…no…Joey, no…he's mine, Mama, he's mine…he's mine! Joey, Joey!

Klausen Move! Move!

Friedrich takes Topthorn to the gun, but Topthorn resists. Klausen tries to manhandle Joey into position. Joey refuses. Klausen goes for Joey immediately with the whip and beats him.

Joey knocks him to the ground; Klausen grabs his gun to protect himself, about to shoot.

Friedrich No, Joey.

Joey might be about to trample Klausen, but Friedrich interposes himself.

[Then to **Klausen**] No!

Klausen I'll shoot him!

Friedrich Don't be an idiot! You need them! You need them!

Klausen Harness them.

The German Soldiers start to harnesses Joey and Topthorn.

Friedrich Good boy. Good boy.

Klausen Don't worry, Müller, you can work my horses. But the day you stop being useful to me I'll put a bullet through your skull. Move.

Friedrich Pull.

Friedrich joins the other German Soldiers to harness Topthorn and Joey.

Scene 8
Continuous, then time passes into October 1918 ('Mud/Hell Scene')

Joey, Topthorn, Heine and Coco pull the gun. Friedrich leads the horses. Klausen drives them.

The team deteriorates progressively…the screen landscape shows time moving and geography changing…

Medium agony of horses and men.

Freeze: 1st exhausted breathing of horses and men.

Enter Song Man.

Song Man Lullee lullay, lullee lullay
My child be not afraid…

Fast agony of horses and men.

Freeze: 2nd exhausted breathing of horses of men.

Till morning gilds the glade, lullay
Till morning gilds the glade…

Slow agony of horses and men.
(Emilie walks off.)

…And two years on, every man and horse is drained. Coco comes out of the traces, wrecked. The team stops.

Soldier (Franz) Lance-Corporal!

Klausen Private, get that horse out of here, back the other one up. Back it up!

Coco coughs and starts to fall. (They have stopped, so the gun sinks into the mud.)

Friedrich	You're driving them to death. Put her out of her misery!

Klausen shoots Coco, expertly, in the heart. Coco squeals in agony. Heine is unhitched, and Joey re-hitched to the gun.

We're slipping in the mud. Stop it! Stop it!

Topthorn coughs, and stumbles.

Friedrich	Topthorn: no, no! *[To a Soldier, now taking control]* Don't harness him!
Klausen	What are you doing?
Friedrich	— You want him for more of your drudgery tomorrow, you rest him now! *[To Soldier, re. Topthorn]* Walk him! Do it!
Klausen	*[Concedes]* Do it…Get us out of here Müller!
Friedrich	*[Exhorts Joey, now the sole horse hitched to the gun]* Joey…it's down to you now, my friend – *[Friedrich's head to the horse's, like Albert]* – I know…I know, my friend, this is damnation. But please, you must pull. *[Gestures to team]* Pull!

Joey tries to pull. No movement.

Get us out of this hell, Joey. Pull!

Joey pulls. And they move. Topthorn, led by the Soldier, follows the gun (or heads off before it). Voices of the village are heard singing a Vorticist version of Rolling Home.

The gun moves forward, and labours off. Heine is left to die. Incoming fire from advancing British.

Coco remains, dead. Heine falls. Enter the carrion crow.

Scene 9
The same: i.e. territory recently vacated by Germans, October 1918 ('British advance scene')

The gun has just disappeared. Dusk. Silence.

*Enter **British Soldiers**, **Sergeant Fine**, **Shaw** and **Roberts**, hunting for the new German positions, wary of finding them, and of ambushes, and booby traps. So they're as silent as possible and don't show lights.*

Albert *is at the head of the column. Since the death of David, he is nervy but a ruthless fighting machine, extacting his revenge on the Germans.*

Albert	…Horse tracks! Look! Fresh ones…deep ruts – a gun.

The platoon assesses the tracks.

Sergeant Fine	Right. Take down our position. Rest here, lads. Three minutes. Shaw, Roberts – sentry.

*The men squat (they don't sit), lean on their rifles, exhausted. One of them records their position. But **Albert** keeps on wandering.*

I said rest.

Albert	I can't, Sarge.

*Suddenly the crow takes flight from **Coco**. It alarms the men.*

Jesus!

Sergeant Fine	You'll give us away, wandering around like a madman!
Albert	These dead horses all over…!

Sergeant Fine	I gave you an order, Narracott, rest!
Albert	We have to take that gun out.
Sergeant Fine	We identify its position. And we report —
Albert	It's only minutes —
Sergeant Fine	You try and do my job one more time, Corporal, and it's bloody Field Punishment Number One!
Soldier	[Re. the position] Done, Sergeant.
Sergeant Fine	Right. End of the break. Move out.
	*One of the sentries (**Shaw**) has spotted **Emilie** – all the soldiers become alert.*
Soldier (Shaw)	– Enemy rear!
Soldier (Roberts)	– Seen! —
Albert	Hold your fire! [Shouts, too loudly] Hold your fire! —
Sergeant Fine	Narracott! —
Albert	– It's a girl…it's a little girl… I won't hurt you…I won't hurt you…It's all right…
	Sergeant Fine blusters in.
Sergeant Fine	Does she speak English? [To **Soldiers**] Anyone speak French?
Albert	What are you doin' all by yourself then, eh?
Sergeant Fine	[Over-enunciating, as to an idiot / child / foreigner] I don't know if you can understand me, love – but have you seen any Jerries?
Albert	You're frightenin' her, Sarge. What's your name? Name? [Gestures] Albert. Albert. You? *Nothing.*

Sergeant Fine	Can't you talk, girl?
Albert	It's all right…calm down…you're a good girl. Good girl.
	Emilie is safe with Albert.
Sergeant Fine	*[To Albert]* Take her back to HQ.
Albert	What? Me?
Sergeant Fine	Yes, you.
Albert	Are you making me do it 'cause I wanted to take out that gun?
Sergeant Fine	No, I'm making you do it 'cause an order's a bloody order!
Albert	But —
Sergeant Fine	That's enough! Get her out of here! If they see us, they'll gas us. Don't hang about.
Albert	Sarge…
Sergeant Fine	Move out.
	They leave Albert and Emilie behind.
Albert	Well, then…
	But Emilie doesn't move, staring at Coco, terrified.
	What is it?
	Emilie makes a couple of steps towards Coco.
	You are right! This horse is moving…she's breathing.
	Emilie indicates that Coco is thirsty and needs to drink. Albert passes his canteen to her. Emilie gives Coco a drink. In the meanwhile Albert inspects the state of the horse.
Albert	This poor mare isn't bon. Can you get up

girl?…Can ya?

Emilie shakes her head.

You know a lot about horses, do you?

Emilie I look for my horse.

Emilie caresses Coco, embracing her head.

Albert You can talk? We can't leave her like this.

But Emilie clings to Coco.

I'm afraid, there's only one thing we can do for her…

Albert takes over, puts Coco's head in his lap, caresses her, Coco snorts and whines in agony.

Turn around, little girl, turn around!

Albert gesticulates, Emilie turns her back on him. Albert talks to Coco soft and tender.

Who are you, poor thing? I had a horse once…

Albert takes out the drawing of Joey, shows it to Coco.

His name is Joey.

Coco wheezes, Emilie looks over her shoulder.

Emilie I follow my horse.

Albert *[To Emilie]* I said, turn around! *[To Coco]* He once was as proud and splendid as you, a noble, noble horse, and now… *[Albert weeps]* Now he's dead.

Albert embraces Coco one last time and then stabs her in the head with his bayonet.

There you go, bon girl. Free now.

Emilie turns around, screams.

She's dead. They are all dead, and I'm effing glad, 'cause what's the point, eh?

Albert looks at the drawing, a long time, kisses it goodbye and puts it down on dead Coco.

Goodbye Joey.

Some gunfire, stray shells and shrapnel in the distance. Albert puts his helmet on Emilie's head to protect her, reaches out for her hand…

Let's go.

But Emilie stands there paralysed.

Emilie   I look for Joey.

A held moment. Gunfire. A big explosion. Followed by the hiss of a gas canister. An incoming cylinder of German tear gas lands with a plop. Emilie screams and exits.

Albert   [With overwhelming rage and despair] Joey! Joey! Joey! Joey!

Enter Song Man.

As Albert wanders blindly upstage, the Song Man sings.

Song Man   And I'll wager a hat full of guineas
Against all of the songs you can sing.
That some day you'll love and the next day you'll lose
And winter will turn into spring
Ploughed, sown, reaped and mown
And the year turns round again.

Scene 10
Behind new German lines,
November 1918

The gun team drags the gun in. The weather is beautiful.

The gun team is halted. They are all exhausted. **Joey** *and* **Topthorn** *are free of their harness.* **Joey** *seems agitated.* **Topthorn** *is more still than usual.*

Friedrich	*[To horses]* Rest for a while, boys. Rest…

On a beautiful day like today, I think of my daughter. I've missed four of her birthdays. And in four years, have we got any closer to Paris? If we're retreating, why don't we just leave this gun here?

Friedrich chats to one of the soldiers. *Klausen overhears.*

Klausen	We're not retreating, it's strategy.
Friedrich	Ah, strategy. The Kaiser's impeccable strategy!
Klausen	Shut up!
Friedrich	Of course, Private.
Klausen	Lance-Corporal!
Friedrich	Lance-Corporal. Sir. *[Mumbled]* Royal imperial Kaiser.
Klausen	What did you say?
Friedrich	I said look at the horses. They're like children.
Klausen	Müller, that's your trouble. You're soft-hearted, and weak, you want to cry because you think they're like children, that they feel as we do. But they are not human, they're beasts, here only to carry us, or pull us. What about the

countless men who've died out here – your comrades? Why for once don't you show some love and pity for them?

Topthorn coughs and their attention is drawn to him. His breath is short and rasping. He coughs again and stumbles.

*Joey makes movements that suggest he's trying to revive **Topthorn**. **Topthorn** falls.*

Topthorn lifts his head to look at Joey.

*Topthorn lies still. **Joey** is distressed.*

*Friedrich listens at **Topthorn**'s chest.*

Friedrich   Topthorn…Topthorn…

We killed you. Noble, noble cavalry horse. You'll never go home. You'll never see Gisa. Damn this war.

*Soldiers aim their guns at **Friedrich**, but **Klausen**, all fight gone, now sees it the same way:*

Klausen   Damn this bloody war.

*Suddenly, an incoming shell lands nearby. Everybody reacts except **Joey** and **Friedrich**. **Klausen** is badly hurt by shrapnel.*

*Another incoming shell. Then a new and terrible sound. Rumbling, roaring. Enter a **German Soldier** (**Schmidt**), fleeing from the direction of the noise.*

Soldier (Schmidt)   Run, run, run!

*Exit all except **Joey**, **Friedrich** and one **Soldier**.*

*Friedrich tries to drag **Joey** away but **Joey** won't budge from **Topthorn**.*

*The **Soldier** shoots in the direction of the terrible sound, but it's no use. He tries to drag*

Friedrich away, but **Friedrich** *won't move. Exit* **Soldier**.

The terrible sound is getting closer. **Joey** *turns his head to listen, but will not leave* **Topthorn**. **Joey** *whinnies to* **Topthorn** *as if to say, "Get up and let's get out of here!"*

A British tank bursts into view and rolls towards them. **Friedrich** *waves for it to stop.*

Machine gunfire from the tank; **Friedrich** *is killed.* **Joey** *puts himself between the tank and* **Topthorn**. *There's a standoff.*

Joey *doesn't budge. The tank advances.*

Joey *challenges the tank. The tank will crush* **Joey**. **Joey** *flees.*

Joey

Scene 11
Joey's night, November 1918

Joey is alone. He runs.

He crosses a river.

He gallops through a farmyard. He jumps a fence.

He clatters through a deserted village. He finds a stream. He drinks.

Night comes. He dozes standing up. He's woken by a white flare.

A machine gun chatters into life. Joey runs again.

A battle starts up next to him in the dark. He runs into barbed wire.

He screams.

His efforts to free himself worsen his injuries. He's limping, in pain.

Every way he tries to limp, the battle breaks out. He's in the middle of it, with nowhere to run.

He is exhausted. Above and around him tracers flicker; lines of red and white and yellow and green. All around him are muzzle flashes, and the flares of explosions.

He half collapses. He might fall.

If he falls he might never rise again.

Suddenly everything stops, the war stops. He doesn't change but around him appears a mist.

Scene 12
No man's land, November 1918

*We begin to glimpse that **Joey** is between opposing positions: Germans one side, British, including **Sergeant Thunder** (now a Regimental Sergeant-Major), the other.*

*A sentry, **Geordie**, begins to glimpse **Joey**.*

Geordie	Stand to! Stand to!
Sergeant Thunder	What is it, Geordie?
Geordie	I thought I saw something moving in no man's land.
Sergeant Thunder	What?
Geordie	Looked like a horse Sarge.
Sergeant Thunder	A horse? Your eyes must be playing tricks on you, you daft Geordie idiot.
Geordie	Honest, Sarge, I saw it.
Sergeant Thunder	There'll be a rum ration in a minute, Geordie. Now keep your eyes peeled for Germans, trez beans? Toot sweet an' all.

*Manfred, a German in the opposing line, glimpses **Joey**.*

Manfred	Quickly!
Soldier (Ludwig)	What is it?
Manfred	A horse!
Soldier (Ludwig)	A horse? Out there in that mud and barbed wire?! You've lost your mind, Manfred.

Laughter.

*This noise from the opposing German line has **Geordie**, at the periscope, out to prove his* *point. The other **British Trenchmen** are still making fun of him.*

__Geordie__ has it as fact now:

Geordie	It's a horse! Sergeant! It's a horse!
Sergeant Thunder	Give me that —

__Sergeant Thunder__ takes the periscope.

Geordie	It's true, lads…
Sergeant Thunder	Well, eff me. A horse out in no man's land.

*That's confirmed it. **Geordie** and others laugh.*

Geordie	Didn't I tell you?!
Sergeant Thunder	Out in that effing bog?! That's unbel – hang about…a white flag.

__Manfred__ is waving a flag, and tentatively climbing out of his position – to some objections from his fellow soldiers: "You can't!", "No, Manfred, do you want to lose your head?" A shot from the British side.

Hold your fire!

British Trenchmen	*[Down the line]* Hold fire! Hold fire!

__Geordie__ fashions a white flag.

Sergeant Thunder	What are you doing?
Geordie	Going for him myself.
Sergeant Thunder	Don't be stupid, Geordie.
Geordie	We can't just let the effing Jerries effing have him.
Sergeant Thunder	Too effing right. One less Geordie in the world, off you go.

__Geordie__ climbs out.

Soldier (Ludwig)	Don't shoot! Don't shoot!
Sergeant Thunder	Hold fire but be prepared!
Manfred	*[To **Joey**, making calming noises as he approaches]* Here…easy…
	*Men from both trenches call to **Joey**.*
Geordie	Hey, bonny lad!
Manfred	Here, boy, here…
	*Etc. **Manfred** and **Geordie** arrive at **Joey**. They concentrate on **Joey**. Help him. This is a novel sight for their comrades – enemies co-operating. When **Joey** is free of the wire, they stare at each other. A quiet descends.*
Geordie	What do we do now?
Manfred	I don't speak English.
Geordie	Two of us and only one horse. We must be careful not to start a war, eh?
Manfred	He's lost a lot of blood.
Geordie	He's bleeding, he needs a vet.
Manfred	I don't speak English.
Geordie	A veterinary surgeon, a doctor, he needs a —
Manfred	Ah, yes, doctor: you mean vet. Yes, yes, we have a hospital behind our lines.
Geordie	*[Over this]* We have one, we have one —
Manfred	What about heads or tails?
Geordie	What?
Manfred	Heads or tails.
	There is another shot from the British side.

British and German Trenchmen	*[Down each line]* Hold fire! Hold fire!
Manfred	Heads…or tails.
Geordie	You mean – heads or tails.

Geordie holds the coin aloft and turns a full circle so both sides can see it.

Heads or tails!

There are shouts of encouragement from both sides.

Manfred	I toss, you call, yes?
Geordie	What?
Manfred	I toss, you call, yes?
Geordie	You toss, Jerry, I'll call.

*Then silence. **Manfred** flips the coin.*

Heads!

Manfred	My name is Manfred. Manfred.
Geordie	Same to you, lad. There's widows weeping everywhere because men couldn't talk like you and I just have.
Manfred	Bonne chance, Tommy.

***Manfred** reveals the coin. **Manfred** hands **Geordie** the reins – cheers explode on the British side.*

Geordie	He's ours, lads! The no man's land horse – it's ours!
Sergeant Thunder	Trez beans, Geordie, trez beans!

*Joey lets **Geordie** lead him.*

*Enter **Song Man** and **Song Woman**.*

Song reprise: **Devonshire Carol**

Song Man/Woman

Tommy in the meadow
Tommy in the byre
Tommy on the firestep
Tommy on the wire
And those who walk in war
And those who walk in peace
And those who walk this blessèd land
Their hope shall never cease.

Scene 13
Behind British lines, November 1918 ('Clearing station scene')

A chaotic clearing station. Wounded men and horses being attended to.

Albert, blinded, eyes bandaged, is being attended to by a nurse, Annie Gilbert. He is having his details confirmed by a matron, Matron Callaghan.

Matron Callaghan: Can you see anything? I said can you see anything?

Albert: No.

Matron Callaghan: Your name is Corporal Albert Narracott, is that correct?

Albert: What does it matter?

Matron Callaghan: Albert, yes? You're lucky it was only tear gas. You will regain your sight. You'll be perfectly all right.

Albert: No, I won't.

Matron Callaghan: The question is, where was your gas mask?

Albert: On my face.

Matron Callaghan	Not soon enough. Well, it's not a Blighty One. Category Two: slight. *[To **Annie**]* Keep an eye on this one. *[To **Albert**]* Nurse Gilbert will see to you.
	Matron Callaghan moves off to another wounded soldier.
Annie	Hello, Corporal. I'm Annie. Don't mind her, she's rather tactless. She's right though, you'll be all right. Now, I'm going to apply some saline…
	*Annie washes **Albert**'s eyes with saline. Dialogue overlaps:*
Albert	I don't want to see…
Annie	I understand, Corporal. Truly, I do.
Albert	…I don't care…
Annie	Sshh…calm down…
	*Enter **Veterinary Officer Martin**. Enter **Joey** with **Sergeant Thunder** and **Geordie**.*
Sergeant Thunder	This, sir, is the no man's land horse.
	*Cheers from the **Soldiers**.*
Geordie	Now it's just his leg, as far as we can see.
Martin	It needs cleaning out, straight away.
Geordie	We sluiced it with water, but we didn't try anything else.
Martin	You did the right thing. Water please.
Sergeant Thunder	Ordinarily we wouldn't be making such a fuss over an injured horse, but the men are talking about him as if he's some sort of miracle.
Geordie	We haven't fed him, in case he needs an operation.

Martin	An operation? He'll be lucky.

Medical supplies are brought and employed.
***Sergeant Thunder** crosses to **Albert**.*

Sergeant Thunder	*[To **Annie**]* What's he got?
Annie	Tear gas.
Sergeant Thunder	*[To **Albert**]* That'll wear off…I said that'll wear off…son? Are you all right, son? What's his name?
Annie	Corporal Albert Narracott.
Sergeant Thunder	Narracott…? Eff me, pardon my French, nurse – I remember a Narracott. There was a Narracott once badgering me about effing horses…pardon my French, nurse. Corporal? That wasn't you, was it?
Martin	It's no use.

*It's true. **Joey** is wrecked. **Martin** checks revolver.*

Geordie	Did you hear that Sarge? He says it's no use.
Sergeant Thunder	That's a shame, that's a damn shame, sir.
Martin	He's half dead and I've got no one to look after him.
Annie	They're putting another poor horse out of its misery…
Albert	I had a horse once.
Annie	So you will speak to me?
Albert	Joey, he was called. Joey.

***Martin** pulls trigger. The gun fails to fire.*

Martin	For god's sake! Gun jammed. Sergeant.

Sergeant Thunder lends his rifle, to objections from the Soldiers.

Thank you.

Martin aims the rifle.

Good boy.

Albert does an owl call. Joey reacts.

What's going on over there?

Annie   Corporal? Corporal, are you all right?

Martin   He's upsetting this horse. Get him away from here, that's an order!

Sergeant Thunder   Nurse! Get him away! Can't you see this is hard enough without upsetting this horse?

Albert   What does he mean, I'm upsetting the horse? What horse?

Annie   The one they're putting down, we've been ordered away —

Albert   Is he answering? Does he know it's me; Albert? Joey?

Joey reacts more. Sergeant Thunder spots this. Martin aims.

Joey wants to go to Albert.

Don't kill him! Don't kill the *bon* horse! Joey! Joey boy!

Sergeant Thunder   Sir, don't pull the trigger —

Albert does an owl call.

Martin   What the hell —?

Joey definitely reacts, taking steps towards Albert.

Sergeant Thunder	Do you see that?
Albert	Joey? Joey boy, is it you?
Sergeant Thunder	It's his effing horse. It's his effing horse from effing home!

***Joey** walks. He and **Albert** find each other.*

Albert	Is it…? It can't be…Is it…? Hello, boy…It's me, Albert. Is it you?

***Albert** blows into **Joey**'s nose. **Joey** blows back.*

Joey. Joey boy! Hello, boy. Hello Joey. Where you bin then, hey? What a dance you've led me. Sorry. Does that hurt? We'll mend that, we will, we will. We'll mend that. You're alive…you're alive. What a *bon* boy.

A bell chimes 11 times, signalling the end of the war, Armistice Day, 11 November 1918. The screen shows the date.

Scene 14
Ted and Rose's farm

Dawn. Birdsong.

*Enter **Albert**, riding **Joey**, the slanting sun behind them. Enter **Rose** and **Ted**.*

*Enter **Song Man** and **Song Woman**.*

Song: *Only Remembered*

Song Man/Woman	Only the truth that in life we have spoken Only the deeds when our journey has run They will pass onward when we are forgotten Only remembered for what we have done Who'll sing the anthems and who'll tell the story?

Will the line hold, will it scatter and run?
Shall we at last be united in glory?
Only remembered for what we have done.

Rose   Eh?

All   Only remembered —

Ted   What is it?

All   Only remembered —

Rose   A man, and a horse…

All   Only remembered for what we have done.

Rose   It can't be —

All   Shall we at last be united in glory?
Only remembered for what we have done
Only remembered for what we have done.

Albert dismounts.

He walks towards his mother. She embraces him.

Ted watches.

The End.

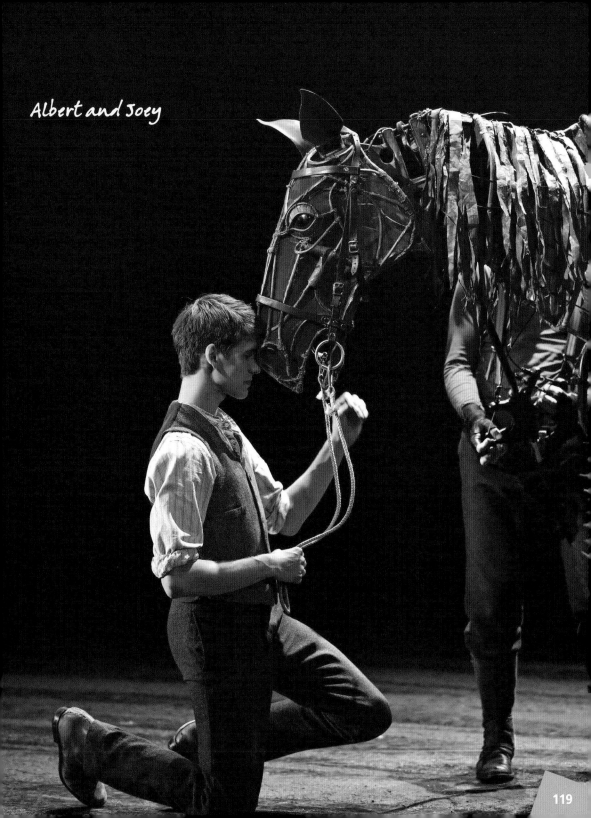

Albert and Joey

Activities

Albert and Joey

Activity 1

Research to understand life during the First World War

Choose one of the following topics to research. You should create a two-minute presentation on your chosen topic that you can then share with the class.

- Key battles of the First World War, for example the Battle of the Somme, the Battle of Verdun or the Battle of Amiens.
- Army regiments such as the Accrington Pals who were recruited from a particular area and fought together.
- The use of horses in the First World War (including their use as cavalry horses and as a means of transporting equipment).
- What life was like for those left at home in Britain during the First World War.
- The 250,000 underage soldiers (like Albert) who fought in the First World War.

Act 1, Scene 1

Activity 2

Create an opening soundscape

The play starts in 1912, two years before the war. In the opening scene, a calm, peaceful atmosphere needs to be created, which will contrast dramatically with the later war scenes.

a. Decide what you would include in a **soundscape** for this scene. Think about:

- sounds you might hear in the country
- how you could use your voices to create a traditional rural atmosphere
- what objects or instruments you might use.

b. If possible, create your own soundscape and record it.

Key term

soundscape
a sound or combination of sounds created as a background to enhance atmosphere or suggest location

Explore alternative ways of presenting Scene 1

There is no speech or **dialogue** in Scene 1. Instead, it is a list of **stage directions**. In the National Theatre production, a sketch of the landscape turns into an animation, then a puppet is used to introduce Joey as a foal. The whole scene could be presented as an animation.

Create a **storyboard** for an animation of this opening scene, like the one started below.

WAR HORSE

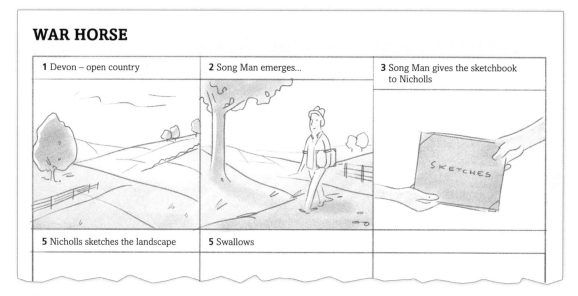

1 Devon – open country	2 Song Man emerges...	3 Song Man gives the sketchbook to Nicholls
5 Nicholls sketches the landscape	5 Swallows	

Key terms

dialogue an exchange of words between two or more characters in a play

stage directions information, usually printed in italics, provided by the playwright about the way in which a scene might be staged

storyboard a planning technique, often used by film-makers, showing a series of sketches or images summarising a scene or sequence of events

Act 1, Scene 2

Write a conversation about the auction

The auction scene reveals a great deal about the characters of Ted Narracott and Arthur Narracott. The auctioneer, Chapman Carter, witnesses everything.

Write a conversation between Carter and his wife about what happened at the auction. Include:

- a description of how Ted and Arthur provoked each other, and the tension between them
- how Carter felt about Albert intervening, to stop his father spending the mortgage money
- how Carter felt about the crowd laughing at the drunk Ted as he tried to catch Joey in the auction ring.

Write the conversation as a playscript. It might start like this:

Mrs Carter	Evening dear, supper will be ready in 10 minutes. How was the auction?
Carter	Evening love. *[He kisses her on the cheek]* What a day! I think we had a record today – thirty-nine guineas for a hunter colt!
Mrs Carter	*[Astonished]* Thirty-nine guineas! Who on earth paid that?
Carter	…

Act 1, Scene 6

Activity 5

Develop a character through hot-seating

Key term

hot-seating
a rehearsal
technique
in which an
actor answers
questions from
the point of
view of the
character they
are playing. It
helps actors
to understand
their character
more clearly

In a rehearsal room, actors might use **hot-seating** to gain insight into characters and their feelings.

a. In groups of three, reread the exchange between Arthur, Billy and Ted in Scene 6 (pages 24-25).

b. Then put each character in turn in the hot-seat and ask them questions. For example, you might ask 'Billy' how he feels about his father and his uncle's poor relationship. You might ask 'Ted' and 'Arthur' what their lives were like as children or what made them fall out in the first place.

Act 1, Scene 8

Activity 6

Experiment with vocal and physical skills to convey emotion

Scene 8 features a lot of heightened emotion as Ted, Albert and Rose argue about the bet that Ted has made. Actors playing the characters in this scene need to use a range of **vocal techniques** and **physical skills** to show the full extent of the emotions that the characters are experiencing.

a. In groups, read through Scene 8 from the beginning to Rose's line 'Both of you, stop it!' (pages 27-29). Then read the scene individually, looking carefully at each speech you have just read aloud as a character.

Choose the most relevant option below for your character and give it a score out of 10:

- level of anger towards another character
- level of fear or concern for themselves
- level of fear or concern for another character.

b. Looking at your scores for each character, decide how you can convey these emotions to an audience through your vocal and physical skills. For example, if you have scored one line with a high level of anger, you might choose to speak it loudly and quickly to demonstrate your anger to another character, and you might move quickly and gesture with your arms to emphasise the point that you are trying to make.

c. Try out your ideas by reading through the scene again with your group, moving around your 'stage' as if in performance.

d. Discuss with your group what worked well and any further improvements you could make.

Act 1, Scene 11

Activity 7

Create a character and summarise their emotions

At the beginning of the war, mustering and sequestering (recruiting men to be soldiers and taking possession of horses for the war effort) was done in an excited, festival-like atmosphere. Everyone believed that the war would be 'over by Christmas'.

a. Decide upon a character who could be part of the crowd in Scene 11. Your character might be:

- a young man who is going to enlist as a soldier
- a mother who doesn't want her son to go to war
- an army officer
- a farmer with a horse to sell
- someone else of your own choosing.

Key terms

vocal techniques methods used by actors to vary their voices to communicate aspects of character. These can include pitch, pace, pause, projection, accent, dialect, volume and tone

physical skills the way in which an actor uses his or her body to communicate character and emotion

Write brief notes about your character, considering the following questions:

- How old is your character?
- Are they, or have they ever been, in the army?
- What is their attitude to the war? Are they excited about the chance to fight for king and country?
- If they are selling a horse to the army, how do they feel about it? Are they worried about how they are going to do farm work without their horse? Are they glad of the money? Do they consider the horse a family pet?

b. Write three sentences that summarise what your character is thinking and feeling:

- at the beginning of the scene
- in the middle of the scene
- at the end of the scene.

c. In the National Theatre production, the crowd scene froze at times, allowing some characters to voice their thoughts. Choose three physical poses to 'freeze' for your character, showing their different emotions. For example, an army officer might stand to attention, or a mother might wipe away a tear. The poses should be relevant for the beginning, middle and end of the scene.

Act 1, Scene 12

Activity 8

Develop interpretive skills through examining facts and asking questions

Key term

interpretation
the choices a director makes about how to present ideas to an audience

Once a director has the script, they need to prepare their own **interpretation** of the play. The director decides what messages and information they want to communicate to the audience, and how they are going to do it. A common preparation technique is a 'facts and questions' activity, in which the director and cast discuss questions and agree on interpretations.

For Scene 12 (pages 49-51), create a table with two columns.

a. In the first column, write down the main facts. This should be information that is clearly included in the text, such as what the characters say and the stage directions.

b. In the second column, write down any questions you have about the scene. These should not ask for information that is explicitly in the text, but for information that a director and actors need to know to decide how they will interpret the play. An example has been started for you, below. You can apply this exercise to any scene in the play.

Facts	Questions
Nicholls tries to reassure Joey when he is startled by gunshot	• How many other horses has Nicholls worked with as a soldier? • Has he always worked with horses, including before he joined the army? • Does he feel sorry for the horses he trains?
The regiment are going to be posted to France the next day	• •

Act 1, Scene 15

Activity 9

Explore persuasive techniques in Major Nicholls' speech

Most speeches in which the speaker is trying to persuade or encourage people to do something use a variety of techniques, such as:

- **alliteration**
- fact
- opinion
- repetition
- **rhetorical questions**
- exaggeration

Key terms

alliteration
the repeated use of the same letter at the beginning of several words

rhetorical question
a question asked in order to create dramatic effect or to make a point, rather than to get an answer

Key terms

imperative
a form of verb that is like a command

emotive language
words and phrases intended to stir up the audience's emotions

- statistics
- triplets (groups of three)
- **imperatives**
- **emotive language**.

a. Find examples of these techniques in Major Nicholls' speech.

b. Which do you think are most effective, and why?

c. Now discuss the following:

- What effect do you think this speech has on the audience in the theatre?
- How does it make them feel about the character of Major Nicholls and the war that the soldiers are fighting?
- Why do you think the playwright has made Major Nicholls sound confident during his speech?

Activity 10

Write a persuasive speech

a. Write a speech to the residents of an English village, asking them to give up their horses for the war effort. Your speech should last no more than two minutes. Try to use as many of the persuasive techniques listed on pages 127–128 as possible.

b. Once everyone has written their speeches, perform them to each other.

c. Which speech is the most inspiring and why?

Act 1, Scene 18

Activity 11

Create an audio performance of a scene

Scene 18 takes place on the battlefield and is one of the most difficult scenes in the play to stage. However, it does lend itself to an audio performance. Working in groups, plan, rehearse and, if possible, record this scene for a radio production.

Think about:

- what type of music you might play
- how you might create appropriate sound effects
- what vocal techniques the voice actors would use to deliver their lines, e.g. pace (speed), pitch (high or low voice), pauses, volume, accent and dialect.

Consider using music, soundscape and a variety of vocal techniques to bring the scene to life and to convey character.

Activity 12

Write a soliloquy for a character

Senior officers could not express fear or doubt to the soldiers in their platoons, but on stage, an actor can reveal their character's true feelings to an audience through a **soliloquy**.

Write a soliloquy for one of the senior officers, focusing on their real feelings about the war and what they are experiencing.

You may wish to consider:

- how the character feels the war is progressing
- how they feel about being responsible for the lives of other men
- whether they are frightened
- how they feel about being away from their family.

Key term
soliloquy a speech in which an actor speaks his or her thoughts aloud

Act 2, Scene 1

Understand the characters' aims

Key terms

objective what a character wants, or what their goal is

verb a word used to describe an action

In the rehearsal room, actors and directors will often work with **objectives** to understand what a character is doing, and why they are doing it. Those objectives are decided by choosing a suitable **verb**, and applying it in the first person. For example, one of the objectives for the actor playing Sergeant Thunder, might be: 'I intimidate Albert'. The objectives change throughout the scene.

a. Read from the beginning of the scene to the end of the first exchange between Sergeant Thunder and Albert 'You spoke again!' (pages 65-66).

b. Look at the lines in the scene listed in the table below and the suggested verbs for finding the character's objective for each of the lines.

c. Choose one of the characters and one of the verbs, then read the lines aloud. The verb you choose should affect the way you say the lines and could change the audience's opinion of a character or situation.

d. Now try the same lines with a different verb. You could also experiment with the lines and verbs of a different character.

e. Discuss which of the verbs works best for each of the lines.

Line	Verbs
Sergeant Thunder: *Bonjour, mes amis!* Spring is in the air. Shame you're not on your Grand Tour of Europe. Nice is very nice this time of year, I'm told. But you're not headed there, and neither am I, more's the pity. Platoon, fall in! Platoon 'shun!	• Intimidate • Entertain • Tease
Albert: What about the horses? My horse went with them, 'e's called Joey, this is his picture, see.	• Question • Inform • Impress

Sergeant Thunder: I don't know where your effing Joey is! Do I look like I know the latest on every effing horse in the war? Do I look like an effing equine expert or even an effing equestrian enthusiast?!	• Humiliate • Dismiss • Reprimand
Albert: But you said there were survivors —	• Beg • Convince • Challenge

Act 2, Scene 2

Activity 14

Explore characters' reactions

Your teacher will allocate one of the following characters to you:

German soldiers	English soldiers	French civilians
Schnabel Friedrich Brandt Klausen	Stewart Bill	Paulette Emilie

Spread out around the room and place a chair in the middle of the room. Your teacher will then read out the following lines from the scene, pausing between each line.

Schnabel   We need this land as a casualty clearing station.

Paulette   This is my land not a German prison!

Friedrich   That British charge was madness.

- The chair in the middle of the room represents the line that is being said. After each line has been read, position yourself in the room depending on how your character feels about the line.
- If you think your character would support what is being said, stand close to the chair and face it. If you think they will strongly disagree, stand as far away from the chair as possible and turn away. For example, even though the line 'That British charge was madness' is spoken by a German soldier, some of the British soldiers may agree with it, so might stand close to the chair.
- Think carefully about your decision and be prepared to justify why you have chosen to stand in a particular place.
- Look around at where other characters have chosen to stand. If you are surprised at any of the decisions, explain why. If you share opinions with your fellow countrymen or with others, explain why.

Act 2, Scene 3

Activity 15

Describe a precious possession

Throughout the play, characters often show particular connection with a precious photograph or object. For Major Nicholls it is his sketchbook. In this scene, David and Albert show each other pictures of those most precious to them.

Imagine that you are another soldier in the crater. Describe a precious object that you might show to the others. It might be a picture or an object with special associations of home, friends or family. You should explain:

- what it is
- what it looks like
- how it came to be in your possession
- how long you have had it
- why it is important to you.

Act 2, Scene 5

Explore staging techniques

In this scene, the **split stage** technique can be used so that the audience can see several different locations and conversations at once. In groups, ideally of seven, stage the scene which involves Rose, Ted and Arthur, David and Albert, Emilie and Friedrich.

a. In your group of seven, read the scene from Albert's line 'I've found a chum called David' to Emilie's line 'Very good, Friedrich! Let's shake hands!' (pages 85–87).

b. Split into subgroups – Albert and David; Ted, Rose and Arthur; Emilie and Friedrich – and rehearse your individual sections. You should think about:

   • where the scene is set and how that affects how much the characters can move around
   • the mood of the scene and the emotions that are being experienced by the different characters.

c. Rejoin your original group and discuss how to fit the sections back together to stage the scene to create a sense of drama. Consider:

   • where each group of characters are on the stage
   • how you are going to direct the audience's attention to the different groups of characters as they speak
   • whether the characters who are not the main focus should freeze while they are not speaking and if so, what position they should freeze in.

d. Perform the full scene extract for the rest of your class.

e. When you have all performed, discuss the following:

   • which of the performances was most effective and why
   • why the playwright has chosen to structure the scene in this way, rather than writing three separate scenes.

Act 2, Scene 11

Write a soliloquy exploring Joey's emotions

In Michael Morpurgo's original novel, Joey is the narrator (he tells the story). In the play, we do not hear any of Joey's thoughts as he is played by a puppet who does not speak.

Scene 11 has no dialogue and is just a series of stage directions describing Joey's troubled journey through one night.

a. Using the stage directions as a framework, write a soliloquy for the character of Joey for this scene. You could include:

- how he is feeling, for example fear or pain
- his opinions about the war
- his observations about the landscape.

b. Perform your soliloquy.

c. Compare the content of your soliloquy with one written or performed by someone else. Identify the similarities and differences. Discuss why you may have interpreted Joey's thoughts differently.

Act 2, Scene 14

Hold a debate about the end of the story

The play ends differently to the novel. In the novel:

- After being reunited with Albert, Joey is sold in an auction in France and is bought by Emilie's grandfather.
- Emilie's grandfather sells the horse to Albert for a penny, making him promise to care for him and love him as much as Emilie did.

- Albert and Joey return home to Devon together and we hear about Albert's marriage and later life.

In the play:

- Albert and Joey are dramatically reunited while Albert is suffering with a temporary loss of sight.
- The play ends with a brief scene where Albert returns to Devon.

a. Debate the statement: 'It was right to change the ending of the play to make it more dramatic', using the steps below.

Step 1

Divide into two groups.
Group A should discuss and draw up arguments agreeing with the statement. Consider issues such as:

- How exactly is the drama improved by changing the ending and making the reunion between Joey and Albert the focus of the end of the play?
- Whether it is acceptable to make changes if it is of benefit to an audience.
- The difference between reading a story and seeing it performed, justifying why changes might need to be made.

Group B should discuss and draw up arguments disagreeing with the statement. Consider issues such as:

- Whether anything is lost by not finding out what has happened to Albert and Joey once they have returned home.
- Whether it is ever acceptable to make changes to an artist's original work.
- The impact on the original artist and how they feel about the work that they have crafted being changed.

Step 2

Appoint a chairperson to oversee the debate. Each side nominates a speaker to put forward the group's arguments. These are presented, then other people are allowed to contribute their ideas. Try to respond to each other's arguments, weighing up the pros and cons.

Step 3

Take a vote on whether it was right to change the ending of the story.

b. Assess how well you performed in this activity. Identify one thing you did well and one thing that you could improve upon when:

- contributing to your group's ideas for the debate
- speaking in the debate and presenting your ideas and viewpoint.

Activity 19

Write a newspaper article about Albert and Joey

At the end of the war, the newspapers displayed triumphant headlines and many published stories of individuals who had displayed great bravery and strength of character.

a. Imagine that you are a journalist interviewing Albert.

- Compile a list of questions that you wish to ask him
- Then imagine that you are Albert, answering those questions. Use all of the information contained in the play to help with your answers.

b. Write an article about Albert and Joey.

You should include:

- an eye-catching headline
- information about Albert, his family and Joey
- details of Albert and Joey's experiences throughout the war
- some general information about the war.

Activity 20

Improvise a new scene

The play ends as Albert and Joey return home to Devon. Albert embraces his mother, but there is no dialogue between them. **Improvise** a short scene between Albert and his parents, where Albert recounts his experiences at war.

Think carefully about:

- the variety of things Albert has seen or experienced (look back through the play to remind yourself of some of these)
- what has happened at home in Devon while Albert has been away and what his parents might want to tell him
- the emotions of each of the characters (Albert might be glad to be home, but may also feel traumatised by his experience and not know how to act in this once-familiar situation).

The whole play

Focus on the theme of 'the universal suffering of war'

Michael Morpurgo says that *War Horse* is about 'the universal suffering of war'. He states the novel is not about winning a war, but about how every side suffers during war.

a. Discuss how the playwright creates sympathy for German soldiers in the play. Consider:

  i. The way in which Friedrich interacts with Joey, Topthorn and Emilie, including:
    • how he talks to them about his life at home and his hopes and dreams for after the war
    • the language that he uses when speaking to them
    • the way in which he defends the more vulnerable characters to his army colleagues.

  ii. The scene in no man's land where the German and British soldiers toss a coin for Joey, including:
    • how the soldiers from both sides recognise Joey's suffering and want to help him
    • the similarities between the groups of soldiers on both sides and how they are portrayed by the playwright.

b. Drawing on ideas from your discussion, write a paragraph explaining how *War Horse* conveys the theme of the universal suffering of war.

Discuss the use of puppets in the play

In the National Theatre production, puppets were used to represent the horses on stage. The horses, especially Joey, have to express many different emotions through the play.

a. Make a list of the different emotions that Joey goes through in the play, from his happiness on the farm with Albert to his fear as he runs through no man's land.

b. Discuss whether you think it is possible to show all of these emotions with a puppet.

- Look at the photographs from the National Theatre production.
- How do you think you could use the puppets and the human actors around them to convey emotion?
- Think about how the puppet can be moved and manipulated and how actors interact with it.
- Is there any other way in which you think the horses could be represented on stage?

Making
the play

War Horse rehearsal

The cast photos in this book are from the *War Horse* performances in London in 2011. *War Horse* was first performed at the National Theatre in London on 17 October 2007 featuring the cast below. This list shows that as well as the actors on the stage, there are many other roles behind the scenes, which you will learn more about in this section.

Cast list

Major Nicholls	Jamie Ballard
Swallow / Emilie	Alice Barclay
Chapman Carter / Rudi	Jason Barnett
Sergeant Bone / Colonel Strauss / Sergeant Fine	James Barriscale
Captain Stewart / Soldat Schmidt	Simon Bubb
Joey's mother, a horse / Goose / Topthorn / Veterinary Officer Martin	Finn Caldwell
David Taylor / Soldat Schultz	Paul Chequer
Song Man	Tim Van Eyken
Young Joey / Topthorn	Thomas Goodridge
Joey's mother, a horse / Dr Schweyk / Coco, a horse / Geordie	Stephen Harper
Rose Narracott / Private Shaw	Thusitha Jayasundera
Veterinary Officer Bright / Karl	Gareth Kennerley
Crow / Joey	Craig Leo
Young Joe / Emilie	Rachel Leonard
Topthorn / Major Callaghan	Tim Lewis
Joey	Tommy Luther
Young Joey / Emilie	Mervyn Millar
Paulette / Crow	Emily Mytton
Swallow / Joey / Crow	Toby Olié
Ted Narracott / Coco, a horse	Toby Sedgwick
Ned Warren / Heine, a horse	Ashley Taylor-Rhys
Albert Narracott	Luke Treadaway
Sergeant Thunder / Soldat Klebb	Howard Ward
Arthur Warren / Soldat Mafred	Alan Williams
Heine, a horse / Ensemble	Matthew Woodyatt
Hauptmann Friedrich Müller	Angus Wright
Directors	Marianne Elliott and Tom Morris
Designer	Rae Smith
Puppet Design & Fabrication	Basil Jones and Adrian Kohler for Handspring Puppet Company
Lighting Designer	Paule Constable

Director of Movement	Toby Sedgwick
Music	Adrian Sutton
Songmaker	John Tams
Music Director	Harvey Brough
Video Designers	Leo Warner and Mark Grimmer for 59 Productions Ltd
Sound Designer	Christopher Shutt
Associate	Mervyn Millar
Company Voice Work	Kate Godfrey, Jeannette Nelson

The photographs used in this play script feature actors from the 2011 production at the New London Theatre, including:

Joey, head	David Grewcock / Stephen Harper
Joey, heart	Shaun McKee / Thomas Wilton
Joey, hind	Emily Cooper / Matthew Forbes
Topthorn, head	Curtis Jordan
Topthorn, heart	Nicholas Karimi
Topthorn, hind	Matt Costain
Baby Joey	Vanessa Faye Stanley, Jack Parker, Ellie Burrow
Paulette	Pascale Burgess
Emilie	Sarah Mardel
Albert	Jack Monaghan
Captain Stewart	William Rycroft
Friedrich	Anthony Shuster
Billy	David Walmsley
Soldiers and ensemble	Danny Dalton, Jack Monaghan, Matthew Forbes, Shaun McKee, Joshua Blake, Eliot Short, Thomas Wilton, Mat Ruttle, Pascale Burgess, Salvatore D'Aquilla

Interview with Marianne Elliott, co-director

Why did you want to direct *War Horse*?

I thought it would be a real challenge. It was incredibly exciting to be adapting a book – I hadn't done that before. I honestly thought that it was almost impossible because the book is written from the horse's perspective – Joey narrates the entire piece. And obviously a talking horse on stage presents a huge challenge.

I met with Tom Morris (the other director of *War Horse*) and I really liked his approach. He's very much from a type of theatre called **physical theatre** and I am from a type of theatre known as **classical theatre** so I knew that whatever happened I would be learning a huge amount about a world I hadn't really delved into previously.

You spent a lot of time developing the production at the National Theatre Studio. How important was it to spend this time workshopping ideas with your team?

It was vital because in a workshop environment you don't have to worry about putting something polished in front of an audience. You can spend time exploring things: how you might approach the structure of the story; how you might physically present a horse growing up from foal to full-grown horse; what a fight between two horses might look like on stage; etc.

In a workshop loads of ideas are explored and eventually some are thrown out and this is also a vital part of the process. I believe nobody can create anything unless they feel safe enough to try and to sometimes fail.

Co-directors Tom Morris and Marianne Elliott in rehearsal

How do you work with the rest of the creative team to create the world of the play?

I often work with people I have worked with before and I think that trust between the team is vital. You need to know that you all understand the process and the hard work required to achieve what you are all working towards.

We would meet after every performance, and every morning we would watch a film of the previous evening's show so that we could agree on ways to perfect the production. The creative team for *War Horse* were all experts in their particular fields and hugely experienced, which meant the collective pool of our knowledge and opinions was far greater than any one person's perspective.

Everyone had something to contribute. For example:

- The lights might tell us what part of the battlefield we were in
- The music might tell us the emotional resonance
- The text would tell us the plot line.

Working in a harmonious way with every single one of these elements (and lots of others) was essential in order for us not to end up telling the story in a conflicted, confusing way.

What were the particular challenges in staging the production?

Aside from the central narrative figure being a horse, some of the main challenges with this production included answering the following questions:

- How do you tell the story of the entire First World War?
- How do you show the span of a horse's whole life?
- How do you develop specific set pieces, for example the battle scene where the cavalry go into fight?

It truly felt like an impossible challenge but it was still enthralling to start down that path.

Why do you think it is important to tell stories like this one on stage?

I think it is important that theatre explores different kinds of worlds and issues in a multitude of ways. I believe it is vital that different peoples' stories are told. Theatre can be a highly creative and inspiring place where the audience collectively dream and imagine by watching a live story unfold in front of them.

We have to keep pushing these boundaries, taking risks – and we have to be supported to do so. Otherwise, theatre will just become solely a commercial venture where it is just about how much money you can make and little else.

Key terms

physical theatre a form of theatre that emphasises physical movement, for example dance, as a way of telling a story

classical theatre a form of theatre that emphasises language as the principal way of telling a story

Interview with Mervyn Millar, puppet co-designer and puppetry director

How did the design of the horse puppets come about?

The design of the puppets happened in response to the development of the script – and the workshopping process also meant that the script would sometimes be rewritten after we saw what was communicated by the actors and puppets working together.

The capabilities of the puppets were first explored in the workshops then subsequently on stage when the play was performed, and later by successive casts. Each new set of puppeteers was able to build on what had gone before.

War Horse rehearsal

Can you tell us about the research into horse behaviour and movement that the puppeteering team did?

We started by observing horse behaviour and reading about it. We made sure to visit horses in different contexts – farm horses, riding school horses and military horses, for example. We wanted the puppeteers to see the differences in how horses behave depending on how they have been trained. We also looked at a lot of video. We wanted to see the most amazing movements horses are capable of and try to replicate them with the puppets.

Most important of all, we tried to get inside the psychology of horses as much as possible. The key to creating believable animals on stage is to ensure they are responsive to what happens around them. We wanted the horses to be improvising on stage as much as possible. The puppeteers needed the relationship between the three of them to understand the mechanisms of the puppet, the mind and instincts of the horse, and the mechanics of movement in a horse's body. Then they could start to play with how their horse might respond to the scene.

So much of the story is reliant on the audience believing in and caring about the horses. How did you ensure that this was the case?

In this context puppetry is just another type of acting – and one which needs to be very specific, using the limits and capabilities of the puppet body instead of those of the actors' own. For the audience to believe in the horse character, the puppeteers needed to imagine it fully themselves. When the three puppeteers fully engaged in imagining their horse as a distinct personality going through these intense emotional experiences, the audience experienced that consistency of character, just as with any good acting performance.

How did you bring the puppets to life?

The puppeteers worked hard on their technique and characterisation but it's not just them who do the creation. The life of the puppet is something that exists in the mind of the audience. It's often said of the puppets in *War Horse* that 'they move just like real horses'. But in fact, although the movement is based on thorough research and observation, the actual movements we used were carefully selected and filtered to make their meaning in the scene clearer than would be the case with a real horse. The puppet designer Adrian Kohler designed them in such a way that certain parts of the body receive more focus – the ears and tail, for example; and the teams of puppeteers are constantly improvising, working to find the right movements to express the shifts in thought and mood that their character is experiencing. The audience take in this information and piece it together to make something that feels very much like a horse.

Did you have to create rules for the puppets and for the actors who interacted with them?

The movements of the puppets are not exactly like real life. Actors, on the other hand, even on stage, usually try to create a style that feels as 'natural' as possible. With these two performance styles happening close together, we needed to find ways to blend the joins. The actors needed to be careful not to move too quickly around the horses, for example, in case they made them seem sluggish. The puppets also can't take the kind of full contact that you might give to a real horse – not only are they delicate, but the puppeteer may well be using their strength to hold the puppet in a particular position – so we need rules about when and how contact and pressure can be applied.

War Horse rehearsal

Interview with Michael Morpurgo, author of the original novel

What inspired you to write *War Horse?*

I live in deepest Devonshire in the small parish of Iddesleigh. Shortly after moving there some 40 years ago, I happened one day to go to The Duke of York, our local pub. I recognised the old man sitting by the fire. Wilf Ellis was one of three old men in the village who I knew had been a soldier in the First World War. We got talking. I knew something of the history of that terrible conflict. I had read the war poetry of Owen and Sassoon and Thomas, I had seen the musical play of *Oh! What a Lovely War*, I had read *All Quiet on the Western Front*, but I had never before spoken to someone who had been there as a soldier. Wilf opened his heart to me that day about how it was. I went to see the two other veterans in the village, one of whom had been 'there with horses' as he said, in the cavalry; another who remembered the horse sale in the village at the beginning of the war. I went to France, to Belgium, to the battlefields, to the cemeteries. The more I thought about it, the more it became a story I had to write.

Why did you want to tell the story through Joey's eyes?

There have been many books set in the First World War, but all or most tell the story from the perspective of one side or the other. I thought, tell the story through the eyes of a British cavalry horse, a farm horse bought at a horse sale in a Devon village, that is taken away to be trained, taken to the front, where he is captured by the Germans, is used to pull ambulances, winters on a French farm, and so he sees, hears and feels the war from all sides. This way the story would tell of the universal suffering in the war, the suffering of men, families, and horses.

And why the name Joey? We had a spirited foal on our farm called Joey. And I liked the sound of the name across a field when I heard him being called in.

How did it feel to see your story on stage?

When Tom Morris (one of the two directors) first proposed the idea of adapting *War Horse* for the stage, with life-sized puppets, I was deeply sceptical. The only puppet horse I had ever seen on stage was a pantomime horse. I could not see how it would work. One glimpse at the work of Handspring Puppet Company showed me that this was an inspired idea. The puppets were miraculous. However, I still thought that the production was unlikely to happen. It took two years of workshopping and rehearsals to bring the play to the stage.

When I saw it on the stage I was overwhelmed by the power of the play, the puppets, the music, the design, the lighting, the sound. Ten years on, every time I see it I am amazed again. It is the intensity of the play that touches the audience, young and old. Yes, my story, and the story of that war, those men, those horses, may have been the seed of the play, but the National Theatre have grown the book, taken it to new heights, and taken it all over the world.

There are some differences between the way the story is told in the novel and the away it is told in the play. Did you feel that these changes were necessary to make the story work on stage?

A book is a book, a play is a play. I knew there would have to be changes of course. Did I agree with them all? No. But then I make books, mostly. The National Theatre makes plays. They always consulted and listened. I went to meetings and rehearsals, argued my corner, played a very small part of the creative process, more and more conscious during that process that theatre-making was a different world. I had great respect and affection for the people working on the show. I hoped they knew what they were doing. They did!

What relevance do you think that the story has to a contemporary audience?

When the book of *War Horse* first came out in 1982, there were those who felt it was not relevant, certainly not to the lives of young people for whom the book was intended, that looking back to an old, mostly forgotten war was pointless, and that anyway surely the time had come to forget. At the time there were wars in the world, but they all seemed far away. They were other people's wars. As the years passed and we became embroiled once again in conflict after conflict, as the coffins came home, as we witnessed the grieving, and the struggle of those wounded by war in mind and body, then the story seemed to resonate more and become painfully relevant to us. As war and the threat of war increases, so does our desire for peace. *War Horse*, the book and the play, is for many an anthem for peace.

War Horse at the National Theatre of China, Beijing, 2015

Context

The First World War

The First World War started in June 1914 and ended in November 1918. In total, more than 9 million people died and over 21 million were wounded. Hostilities started in Europe between two countries, Serbia and Austria-Hungary. Within a few weeks, some of the most powerful countries in Europe had joined in, including Britain, France and Germany, and by the time the war ended in 1918, twenty-eight countries in six continents were involved. The war was fought on land, at sea and in the air, using the latest tactics and weapons technology that were available at the time.

War Horse is set on the Western Front, the line of trenches that stretched from the English Channel all the way through Belgium and France to Switzerland. As a stalemate set in on the Western Front, other fronts opened up around the world in the effort to defeat Germany and her allies.

The Battle of the Somme, October 1916: a twelve horse team taking the big gun up to the front line

Horses in the First World War

Although the First World War is sometimes described as the first 'modern' war, in 1914 the use of motor vehicles was not widespread so all sides still relied on horses. Early on in the conflict, the cavalry (soldiers who fought on horseback) were involved in some attacks on enemy lines but these attacks were made impractical as the war went on because of trench warfare, barbed wire and machine guns. Horses and mules were still invaluable as a means of moving supplies, ammunition and artillery to the front line, and pulling field kitchens and ambulances.

More than 8 million horses and mules died during the First World War on all sides; Britain alone lost over 484,000 horses, killed by gunfire, poison gas or aeroplane bombs.

*keepers and their messenger dogs
at the British War Training School*

Thousands more were left lame by nails and blades on the battlefield.

So many horses were needed during the war that they were in short supply. From 1914 onwards they were shipped across from North America to boost the ranks of the British Army. During the course of the conflict, the British Army sent almost 6 million tonnes of fodder for the horses on the Western Front. This was slightly more than the weight of ammunition sent, but it was never enough for all the animals.

Care of the horses was also a problem. Many of the soldiers were inexperienced horsemen and didn't know how to ride or look after the animals properly. Horses were often overloaded, became saddle sore or were made ill through the wrong kinds of food being given to them.

Other animals in the First World War

Horses weren't the only animals to be used in the First World War.

- Messenger dogs were used to communicate information between different lines.

- Mercy dogs were used to seek out injured soldiers and would carry first aid supplies.

- Pigeons were used to relay information across the battlefield.

- In the Middle East, camels were used in roles filled by horses and mules on the Western Front.

Timeline of the First World War

1914

June
Assassination of Archduke Franz
Ferdinand, heir to the throne of Austria-
Hungary by members of Black Hand.

July
Austria-Hungary declares war on
Serbia – the first countries are now
at war in what would become the
First World War.

August
Within the space of a week, Russia
steps in to support Serbia; Germany
declares war on Russia; France moves
to support its ally Russia and Britain
declares war on Germany. Germany
invades first Belgium and then France.

September Stalemate at the Battle
of the Marne (northern France); the
'Race to the Sea' begins: both sides try
to reach the English Channel first to
outflank each other.

November
British declare the North Sea a 'War
Zone' and that any ships entering it
do so at their own risk.

1915

February
The Gallipoli Campaign begins in
Turkey when British and French ships
attack Turkish forts at the entrance to
the Dardanelles.

April
The first use of poisoned gas.
Also, Italy joins the conflict on Britain
and France's side.

*Chemical warfare
using poisoned
gas in the First
World War*

December
General Sir Douglas Haig takes control
of British forces on the Western Front.
The Gallipoli Campaign ends.

February **1916**
Battle of Verdun begins, the war's longest battle.

May
The Battle of Jutland, the war's only large-scale naval battle.

July
The Battle of the Somme begins, the First World War battle that involves the most soldiers.

September
Tanks first used in battle, during the Somme Offensive.

1917

February
German submarines re-start a series of U-boat attacks on Allied shipping.

March
The first of two Russian Revolutions takes place.

April
The USA joins the conflict on Britain and France's side.

July
The Battle of Passchendaele (or the Third Battle of Ypres) begins.

November
Second Russian Revolution.

March **1918**
Treaty of Brest-Litovsk between Russia and Germany officially ends Russia's role in the war.

April
French army leader, Ferdinand Foch, becomes Supreme Allied Commander.

August
The Allied counter-attack (later known as the 'Hundred Days') begins.

November
Germany fighting alone after the surrender of her allies. The German emperor, with his country in chaos, abdicates (gives up his office). The government that replaces him asks for an armistice (ceasefire), which begins at 11am on 11th November.

October
German sailors based in Kiel refuse to follow orders. News of their mutiny begins to spread to other German ports and towns.

Glossary

alliteration the repeated use of the same letter at the beginning of several words, e.g. Peter Piper Picked a Peck of Pickled Peppers

classical theatre a form of theatre that emphasises language as the principal way of telling a story

dialogue an exchange of words between two or more characters in a play

emotive language words and phrases intended to stir up the audience's emotions

hot-seating a rehearsal technique in which an actor answers questions from the point of view of the character they are playing. It helps actors to understand their character more clearly

imperative a form of verb that is like a command

improvise create and perform a scene without detailed preparation or rehearsal

interpretation the choices a director makes about how to present ideas to an audience

objective what a character wants, or what their goal is

physical skills the way in which an actor uses his or her body to communicate character and emotion

physical theatre a form of theatre that emphasises physical movement, for example dance, as a way of telling a story

rhetorical question a question asked in order to create dramatic effect or to make a point, rather than to get an answer

soliloquy a speech in which an actor speaks his or her thoughts aloud

soundscape a sound or combination of sounds created as a background to enhance atmosphere or suggest location

split stage the stage is divided into two halves (left and right). Two different scenes are played out in front of the audience, but they may be connected in some way. For example, a character having a nightmare may have the character 'asleep' in bed on one side of the stage, while other actors show the dream the character is having on the other side

stage directions information, usually printed in italics, provided by the playwright about the way in which a scene might be staged

storyboard a planning technique borrowed from film-making, which shows a series of images or shots seen by the audience

verb a word used to describe an action

vocal techniques methods used by actors to vary their voices to communicate aspects of character. These can include pitch, pace, pause, projection, accent, dialect, volume and tone